YORKSHIRE

A pictorial guide to favourite places

Sketchbook

Malham signpost

Jim Watson

SURVIVAL BOOKS • BATH • ENGLAND

A pretty corner of Robin Hood's Bay

First published 2015

Survival Books Limited
Office 169, 3 Edgar Buildings,
George Street, Bath BA1 2FJ, United Kingdom
Tel: +44 (0)1225-462135
email: info@survivalbooks.net
website: www.survivalbooks.net

British Library Cataloguing in Publication Data
ACIP record for this book is available
from the British Library.
ISBN: 978-1-909282-77-3

Front cover illustration: Burnsall in Wharfedale

Printed in China by D'Print Pte Ltd

CONTENTS

Hole of Horcum, North York Moors

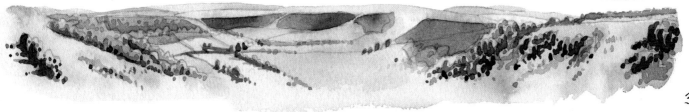

3

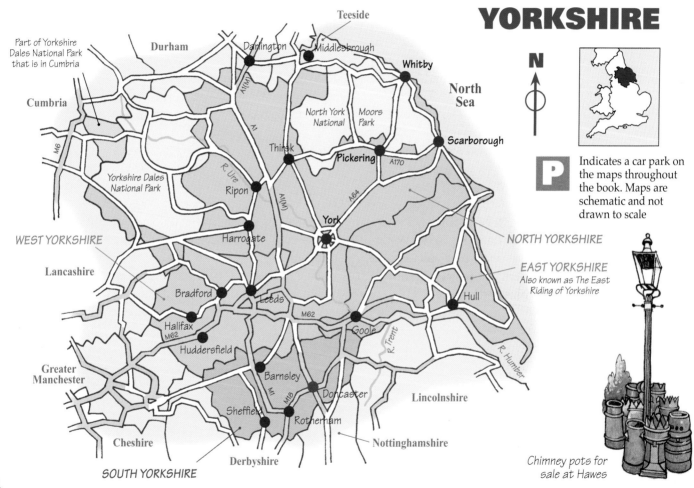

YORKSHIRE

N

P Indicates a car park on the maps throughout the book. Maps are schematic and not drawn to scale

Part of Yorkshire Dales National Park that is in Cumbria

Durham

Cumbria

Darlington

Teeside

Middlesbrough

Whitby

North Sea

North York National

Moors Park

Scarborough

Thirsk

Pickering

A170

R. Ure

Ripon

A1(M)

A64

York

Yorkshire Dales National Park

WEST YORKSHIRE

Harrogate

NORTH YORKSHIRE

Lancashire

M6

A1

A1(M)

EAST YORKSHIRE
Also known as The East Riding of Yorkshire

Bradford

Leeds

Hull

Halifax

M62

M62

Goole

R. Trent

Huddersfield

Greater Manchester

Barnsley

M1

M18

Doncaster

Lincolnshire

R. Humber

Sheffield

Rotherham

Cheshire

Derbyshire

Nottinghamshire

SOUTH YORKSHIRE

Chimney pots for sale at Hawes

4

INTRODUCTION

It's easy to scoff when you hear that 'Yorkshire has everything', especially when said by a Tyke (Yorkshire person) but the more I explore this vibrant and diverse county the more I'm convinced that it's true. The county is the largest in the UK, which helps if you have to fit everything in, but there's still space for the wild areas where you can walk all day and hardly meet anybody else.

Yorkshire abounds in stunning vistas across rolling fields, hills and beaches. There's breathtaking rivers, cliffs, dales and moorland to explore. It boasts five national museums, three national parks, three UNESCO sites, a stunning coastline and seven vibrant cities. With World-class attractions, historic houses and castles, picturesque villages, fine restaurants, vibrant culture, abundant shopping, cricket, fish and chips and real ale, there's truly something for everyone.

The Yorkshire folk I met travelling round were unfailingly friendly, helpful and funny. I never had any problem getting them to talk. Shutting them up was another matter.

A book of this size couldn't possible cover all of the county so it concentrates on the two national parks – the Yorkshire Dales and the North York Moors, plus the city of York. Nobody should ever tour North Yorkshire without going to York.

The places I've chosen to illustrate are my own favourites, some were new to me but the majority I've been to before. None of them were a disappointment and I'll go back to all of them again at the drop of a flat cap. Most are popular tourist destinations, so you'll probably find some of your own favourites amongst them.

This book will tell you how you can drive to each place, where you can park, some relevant history and what to look out for. I also hope that it not only informs, but also entertains and, if you're a visitor, gives you something to enjoy when you're back home.

What it can't do is provide the unexpected surprise that will stay with you forever. You have to experience those for yourself. I've enjoyed many of them on my travels throughout this remarkable county. I do hope you will too.

Jim Watson

Rugby, 2015

Reeth doorway

5

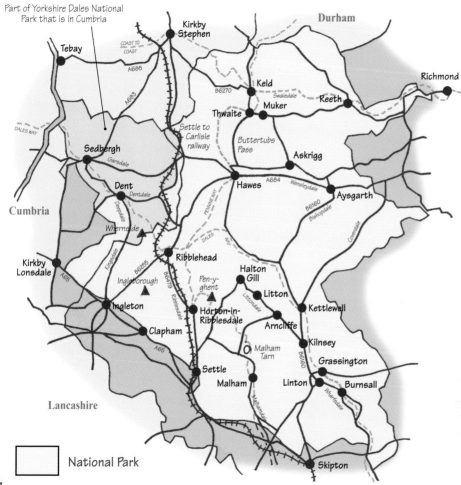

Part of Yorkshire Dales National Park that is in Cumbria

Durham

Tebay

Kirkby Stephen

COAST TO COAST

A685

A683

Richmond

DALES WAY

B6270

Keld

Swaledale

Muker

Reeth

Thwaite

Settle to Carlisle railway

Buttertubs Pass

Askrigg

Sedbergh

Garsdale

Dent

Dentdale

Hawes

A684

Wensleydale

Aysgarth

Cumbria

PENNINE WAY

B6160

Bishopdale

Coverdale

Whernside

Deepdale

Kingsdale

DALES WAY

Kirkby Lonsdale

A65

Ribblehead

B6255

B6479

Ribblesdale

Inglaborough

Pen-y-ghent

Halton Gill

Litton

Littondale

Kettlewell

Ingleton

Horton-in-Ribblesdale

Arncliffe

Clapham

A65

Kilnsey

Grassington

Malham Tarn

Settle

Linton

Burnsall

Malham

Malhamdale

Wharfedale

Lancashire

National Park

Skipton

Yorkshire Dales National Park

- Established in 1954
- Covers an area of 680 square miles
- 95% privately owned
- Over 12 million day visitors a year
- Local population of over 20,000
- Over 900 miles of footpaths
- About 385 miles of bridleways
- Some 5,400 miles of drystone walls
- More than 630 miles of hedgerow
- Over 1,000 species of moths, around 100 species of nesting birds, over 25 species of butterflies and more than 30 species of mammals

Settle doorway

YORKSHIRE DALES NATIONAL PARK

There's nowhere quite like the Yorkshire Dales. It's truly wonderful countryside that can change from pastoral idyllic valleys to dramatic limestone uplands in a mile or so, often in the same dale.

The National Park covers a large slice of the western side of the county of North Yorkshire with, confusingly, part of Cumbria. It contains Yorkshire's three highest mountains, Pen-y-ghent, Ingleborough and Whernside. With a geological make up of mainly porous limestone that's scoured by numerous rivers and streams, the area abounds in potholes, caves, sinkholes and waterfalls.

There's more than twenty dales with three of the main ones, Wharfedale, Ribblesdale and Malhamdale, running roughly north to south. Swaledale and Wensleydale cross west to east. Most take their names from rivers that run through them or a main town or village.

The lower dales are generally green and pastoral with pretty villages, while the upper ones are more austere with small scattered settlements. Roads run along the valley bottoms following the rivers then become narrow and unfenced as they cross high moorland into the next dale. Each dale has its own individual character and it's the amazing variety of terrain that gives this unique area its special appeal.

Typical Swaledale scenery

7

Market Place is still at the centre of the town's activities, where a market is held on Tuesdays.

An unusual three-storey building, the Shambles, overlooks the square. It was originally a 17th-century row of butchers shops. The arches were added in the 18th century with, most unusually, a terrace of two-storey houses built across the top.

Market Place

SETTLE RIBBLESDALE

The main market town of Ribblesdale, Settle sits snuggly in the shadow of Castleberg, an impressive limestone outcrop and a fantastic viewpoint for an aerial view of the town and the surrounding rolling hills.

Settle prospered during the 17th century as pack horse routes through the Dales brought trade. Wealthy farmers and traders built stone houses and cottages which have survived until today. Inns and Georgian mansions were built after the establishment of the Kendal to Keighley turnpike in the 18th century brought the coach trade. The town has been bypassed since 1988 taking the heavy A65 traffic away from the narrow streets.

With all the facilities you'd expect from a bustling market town, Settle has a workaday charm that's blessedly unspoilt by modern tourism.

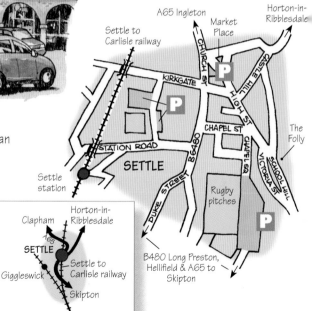

8

Settle's most unusual building is The Folly, a huge, rambling extravaganza of Tudor masonry and exotic window designs, totally out of place amongst the restrained Dales architecture.

It was built during the 17th century on the then main road out of town by local lawyer Richard Preston, who obviously knew how to make an impact with his house. After being empty for over 250 years, which prompted the name of 'The Folly', it was restored in the 1950s. Part of the building now houses the Museum of North Craven Life. The north wing has been painstakingly restored and is let as a luxury holiday apartment.

One of Settle's interesting yards

The Folly

Apart from its setting and the old buildings Settle is probably most famous as the start of the Settle to Carlisle Railway (page 16). Settle station is a superb example of the 'Derby Gothic' style of railway architecture and beautifully kept.

It's like you've stepped back in time – until a pulsating modern diesel train glides in. When it's a steam train – WOW!

Electricity has been generated on the Ingleborough Estate since 1893. There's an operating water turbine-powered generator at the top of the village next to the waterfall, installed in 1948.

Originally it supplied the church, Ingleborough Hall, Home Farm and 13 street lights. There's another working turbine in the sawmill, although it's now augmented by an electric motor when the larger saw is in use.

The New Inn Hotel and Clapham Beck

CLAPHAM RIBBLESDALE

Bisected by tree-lined Clapham Beck, the picturesque village of Clapham is set on a gentle slope just off the A65. Four attractive bridges cross the beck within around 500 yards.

The Farrer family have lived here since the 18th century, establishing the Ingleborough Estate which includes much of the village. They planted many of the wonderful trees and dammed the beck creating a lake north of the village.

Drawn by Clapham's attractiveness and limestone features, the village is generally busy with walkers, potholers and families. A large car park, some small shops and tea rooms caters to them. The New Inn, an 18th-century coaching inn, offers accommodation, a slap up meal or quiet refreshment.

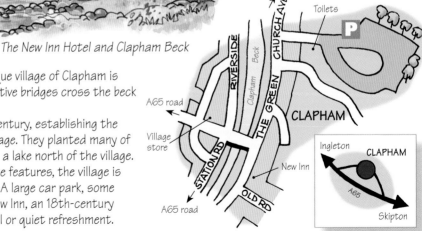

The village store and 'Clapham Rocks' emporium, selling gemstones, minerals, crystals and fossils

Clapham lies on the Craven Fault, a geological feature where underlaying millstone grit and limestone meet creating an abundance of potholes and caves.

A 10.5 mile underground river system begins on the slopes of Ingleborough and ends in Ingleborough Cave just north of the village. The cave was unknown until 1837, when a great storm washed away debris blocking the entrance.

Tours with an expert guide take visitors to view the remarkable limestone formations. These are add-ons to the Ingleborough Estate Nature Trail, which is accessed up the road past the church. The tour of just over a mile takes in old saw mills, hydro-electric installations, woodland and many striking limestone scars.

One of the Farrer family was the notable botanist, Reginald (1880–1920), who collected many species of rhododendrons, shrubs and alpines in China, Tibet and Upper Burma between 1914 and 1920. The fruits of his labours can be seen on the estate nature trail.

The church of St James was founded in Norman times and originally dedicated to St Michael. It's mentioned in records dating back to 1160. Clapham and the church were burned during a Scottish raid following the Battle of Bannockburn in the early 14th century. The tower was probably erected following this incident, but the rest of the church dates from the 19th century.

St James's Church and the road to Ingleborough Cave

11

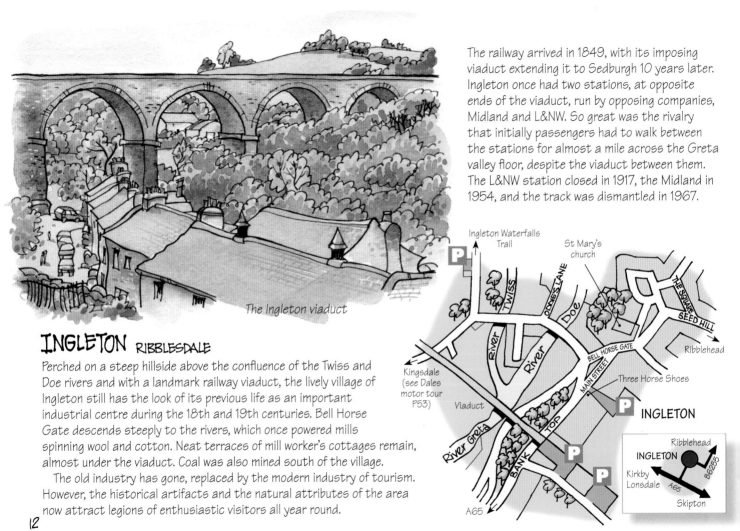

The railway arrived in 1849, with its imposing viaduct extending it to Sedburgh 10 years later. Ingleton once had two stations, at opposite ends of the viaduct, run by opposing companies, Midland and L&NW. So great was the rivalry that initially passengers had to walk between the stations for almost a mile across the Greta valley floor, despite the viaduct between them. The L&NW station closed in 1917, the Midland in 1954, and the track was dismantled in 1967.

The Ingleton viaduct

INGLETON RIBBLESDALE

Perched on a steep hillside above the confluence of the Twiss and Doe rivers and with a landmark railway viaduct, the lively village of Ingleton still has the look of its previous life as an important industrial centre during the 18th and 19th centuries. Bell Horse Gate descends steeply to the rivers, which once powered mills spinning wool and cotton. Neat terraces of mill worker's cottages remain, almost under the viaduct. Coal was also mined south of the village.

The old industry has gone, replaced by the modern industry of tourism. However, the historical artifacts and the natural attributes of the area now attract legions of enthusiastic visitors all year round.

Ingleton Waterfalls Trail

St Mary's church

THE SQUARE

SEED HILL

Ribblehead

Kingsdale (see Dales motor tour P53)

Bell Horse Gate

Three Horse Shoes

Viaduct

INGLETON

BANK TOP

MAIN STREET

River Greta

A65

Ribblehead

INGLETON

Kirkby Lonsdale

A65

B6255

Skipton

Ingleton streets are narrow and winding, centred on a tiny market place. There's a good selection of independent shops with an hospitable pub at each end of the main street.

The parish church, dedicated to St Mary the Virgin, stands high above the river on an unstable foundation of boulders and sediment which had to be strengthened with concrete in 1930 and 1946.

The Norman font is dated at around 1150, the tower is 15th-century and the nave was rebuilt towards the end of the 19th century to a design by the then vicar.

The two-level village and St Mary's church

The Ingleton Waterfalls Trail is one of the village's main attractions. A four and a half mile walk, the Trail follows a well-defined footpath over moderately inclined ground, with steps whenever there's a climb. It boasts some of the most spectacular waterfall and oak woodland scenery in the country.

Ingleton is also a popular start for an ascent of Ingleborough, one of the famous 'Three Peaks' (see p18).

The writer Arthur Conan Doyle was a regular visitor to the area and was married locally, as his mother lived at Masongill from 1882 to 1917. It's possible that he may have been inspired for the name of his famous fictional detective by the vicar – and nave designer – of St Mary's (1874-79) who was called Cornelius Sherlock.

Main Street

13

HORTON-IN-RIBBLESDALE

Though pleasant enough, compared with its more glamorous neighbours in Ribblesdale, Horton is a rather ordinary village. However, it does attract a huge number of visitors, mainly walkers heading for Pen-y-ghent.

Travelling north on the B6479 Horton is the last outpost of rolling green fields before bleak and empty moorland take over.

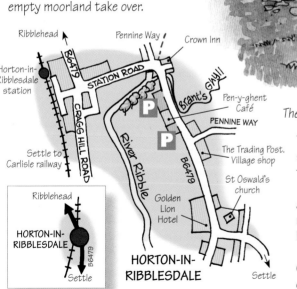

The Crown Inn and Pen-y-ghent

The village straggles along for a mile or more between a series of three sharp bends in the road. There's a small shop and two pubs – the Crown at the north end and the Golden Lion at the south.

Horton has a long history of limestone quarrying and there are the scars across the hillsides to prove it. The Settle to Carlisle railway runs along a rock shelf above the village and its arrival during the 19th century greatly bolstered the industry.

These days Horton is an important walking, climbing and potholing centre. Cyclists also stop here to refuel. The Pen-y-ghent Café in the village is the official headquarters for the Three Peaks Walk (see page 18).

Grey-stoned and squat-towered, St Oswald Church sits easily in the rural landscape. The view of Pen-y-ghent from the churchyard has become a much-photographed classic. With a complete Norman nave, south door and tub-font, St Oswald's is the most complete of all the Norman churches built in the Yorkshire Dales after the Norman Conquest. The square tower was built later. The lychgates into the churchyard are roofed with slabs of Horton slate.

Golden Lion Hotel

St Oswald's Church and Pen-y-ghent

Bridge over the Ribble

A car park near the Crown fills up quickly, especially in summer. People parking on the streets while off on all-day leisure activities are hugely unpopular with residents. However, the huge influx of visitors has radically changed Horton's fortunes. From being a isolated rural community it has now become an outdoor leisure hotspot.

The Station Inn

RIBBLEHEAD

Viaduct · Farm Track · Roadside parking · Hawes · Station Inn · Horton-in-Ribblesdale · Ribblehead station · Ingleton

Hawes · Ingleton · RIBBLEHEAD · Ribblehead station · Horton-in-Ribblesdale

RIBBLEHEAD RIBBLESDALE

CARLISLE
Armathwaite
Lazonby
Langwathby
APPLEBY
Only Carlisle, Appleby and Settle stations are manned
Smardale Viaduct
Kirkby Stephen
Garsdale
Aisgill summit
Dent
Arten Gill Viaduct
Denthead Viaduct
Blea Moor Tunnel
Ribblehead
Ribblehead Viaduct
Horton
Clapham
Carnforth
SETTLE
Giggleswick
Skipton

The Settle to Carlisle Railway

Set in a moorland wilderness of few fields, trees or even sheep, Ribblehead is on the loneliest stretch of railway in England, the Settle to Carlisle line. Thousands of people visit this spot with only one thing in mind – to see the viaduct, and if they're really lucky a steam train crossing it.

First sighting can be an overwhelming and emotional experience. From any direction, in any weather, the curve of the viaduct looks wonderful.

The Midland Railway company completed the line in 1876. Climbing to a height of 1,169ft (356m) at Aisgill summit it's one of the great Victorian feats of engineering, with 20 major viaducts and 14 tunnels along the 72 miles of track – built using primitive tools, muscle and dynamite. Of the 1,000 navvies employed over 100 were killed.

Rivalling its construction have been the epic battles to keep the line open. The Beeching Report closed stations in 1970 and British Rail proposed a total closure in the early 1980s. This caused such an outcry the plan was shelved in 1989 and stations were reopened to meet the new demand.

Ribblehead is now a major tourist attraction but there's no gift shop, admission tickets or barriers. You can walk underneath the arches. Hooray!

The Station Inn, the only building around, copes valiantly with the crowds and even provides a bunkhouse if you want to stay overnight.

Ribblehead viaduct was designed by engineer, John Sydney Crossley. The first stone was laid on 12 October 1870 and the last in 1874. The viaduct is 440yds (400m) long, and 104ft (32m) above the valley floor at its highest point. It has twenty-four arches of 45ft (14m) span, with foundations 25ft (8m) deep. The north end of the viaduct is 13ft (4m) higher in elevation than the south. Some of the limestone blocks weighed 8 tons and 1.5 million bricks were used in the construction.

Dent station – 1,150ft (350m) above sea level, the highest mainline station in England and one of the most remote

A steam train crosses the viaduct with Whernside in the background

17

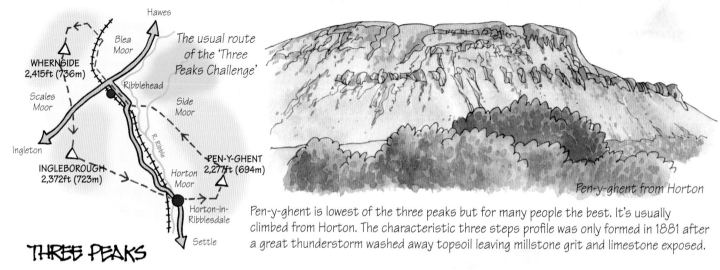

The usual route of the 'Three Peaks Challenge'

WHERNSIDE
2,415ft (736m)

Hawes

Blea Moor

Ribblehead

Scales Moor

Ingleton

INGLEBOROUGH
2,372ft (723m)

Side Moor

R. Ribble

Horton Moor

PEN-Y-GHENT
2,277ft (694m)

Horton-in-Ribblesdale

Settle

Pen-y-ghent from Horton

Pen-y-ghent is lowest of the three peaks but for many people the best. It's usually climbed from Horton. The characteristic three steps profile was only formed in 1881 after a great thunderstorm washed away topsoil leaving millstone grit and limestone exposed.

THREE PEAKS

Though mere pimples in the ranking of English mountains, (even calling them 'peaks' is a typical Yorkshire exaggeration) the Three Peaks – Whernside, Ingleborough and Pen-y-ghent – dominate this wild and desolate area, which is totally unlike any of the green, verdant dales. The peaks stand alone in the landscape, their destinctive shapes making them instantly recognisable – even, with a bit of prompting, for tourists.

They are a venue for numerous walks, runs and cyclo-crosses. The most popular challenge is to complete an almost 25 miles circuit, climbing all three in under 12 hours. The Pen-y-ghent Café in Horton houses a clocking in/out machine which determines whether they've been climbed within the allotted time. The footsore walker is awarded membership of the Three Peaks of Yorkshire Club – and hopefully a nice cup of Yorkshire tea.

The Pen-y-ghent Café in Horton

CAFE

Whernside lacks the good looks of the other two but as the loftiest it's a must-climb hill. Since extensive footpath construction the route from Ribblehead is straightforward, still challenging, but for some, unexciting. The view from the summit is far-reaching. On a clear day you can see Morecambe Bay and – with binoculars – Blackpool Tower.

Ingleborough, has a characteristic flat top appearance, with turret-like outcrops and tiers on the flanks, making it recognisable from any direction. The ascent from Ingleton is relatively easy, though rather tedious, but with a steep climax onto the top. The summit is a broad plateau, a half mile in circumference, carpeted with dry turf and once the site of a huge Iron Age fort.

Whernside

The record for the fastest completion of the Three Peaks Challenge is 2 hours 29 minutes and 53 seconds, which has stood since 1976. The woman's time, recorded in 1996, is 3 hours, 16 minutes and 17 seconds.

Needless to say neither runner wasted any time looking at the view, taking selfies or picnicking on a summit!

Ingleborough from Ribblehead, the famous 'blue' side which is usually in shadow

19

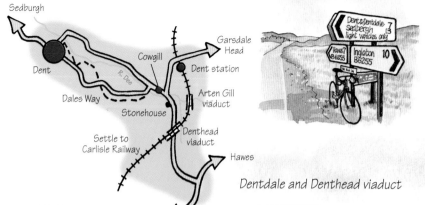

Near Cowgill a minor road climbs to unmanned Dent station, set in wild and windswept moorland with sensational views back to the dale and across the surrounding fells. Though called Dent station, it's actually four miles from Dent village. When the station was reopened for trains in 1986, Railtrack sold the station buildings. Now tastefully renovated, they can be hired for self-catering holidays with a difference.

Dentdale and Denthead viaduct

DENTDALE

Though one of the shorter Yorkshire Dales, Dentdale – named after the only village of any size in the dale – is also one of the most beautiful. The valley is a haven of peace and tranquility. The River Dee runs most attractively through it in a succession of small waterfalls with the road running alongside.

The steep descent into the dale from the B6255 provides fabulous views, particularly of the Denthead viaduct which the road goes under further down the steep hill. Expect to meet walkers and cyclists as this is part of the Dales Way and Dales Cycle Way.

20

Denthead viaduct and resting cylists

Denthead viaduct has 10 arches, is 100ft (30m) high and 199yds (183m) long. The viaduct was built between 1869 and 1875 for the Midland Railway Company using massive blocks of Dent marble and spans the quarry that produced it.

Arten Gill is the larger of the two viaducts in the dale, having 11 arches rising to 117ft (36m) high and is 220yds (200m) in length. It's also built of blocks of Dent marble from now-disused quarries nearby. The stone was popular for ornamental masonry and remarkable for its wealth of fossils.

The viaduct is featured in a scene in the film, *Miss Potter*, the Beatrix Potter biopic starring Renee Zellweger, as she travelled from London to the Lake District. Going through Dentdale to the Lakes would in reality have been possible, but would have been a seriously indirect route.

Small settlements and farms are scattered around the dale, with the Sportsman's Inn at Cowgill the only facility before reaching Dent. The country inn is steeped in history going back over 350 years. Drovers taking livestock to market stayed here, as did navvies working on the Settle Carlisle railway line. The welcoming tradition continues, with today's tourists, walkers and cyclists invited to stop and sample the quality food and ales available.

The Sportsman's Inn

The village from the Cowgill road

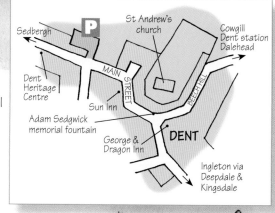

DENT DENTDALE

With the looks of a Cornish fishing village and set in the Yorkshire Dales National Park, it's surprising to find that Dent is actually in Cumbria. This village is totally surprising. Its cobbled streets are narrow and winding, lined by sturdy white-walled cottages with colourful gardens. Tottering chimneys on dark low-pitched roofs are set against distant green hills. For such a pretty dale, Dent is the perfect village. A large car park and a caravan site are testament to its popularity with tourists. There are a few shops and tea rooms, and it's the venue for a number of beer and folk festivals in summer.

During the 17th & 18th centuries the first floors of many cottages were spinniing galleries, where women spun yarn from local sheep wool. A thriving cottage industry developed knitting simple garments, which continued until the late 19th century. 'The terrible knitters of Dent' – terrible in the sense that they were terribly good – were renowned for their skill and speed. So fast that their needles often became bent.

You can learn all about the knitters at the Dent Village Heritage Centre, which tells the story of Dent through the working lives of Dales' folk with many exhibits. The centre itself was designed and built entirely by local labour, beautifully converted and extended on the site of a disused filling-station, opposite the car park.

A Dent cottage

The 12th-century Church of St Andrew has Norman features in the tower and arched doorway. Dent is the birthplace of Professor Adam Sedgwick (1785-1873), the great Victorian geologist and contemporary of Darwin. The son of the then vicar, Sedgwick attended the old Free Grammar School on the north-west edge of the churchyard. He went on to be a boarder at Sedbergh School before going up to Trinity College, Cambridge. For all his importance as a geologist, Sedgwick remained a son of the Dales and a water fountain made from a rough-hewn block of pink Shap granite stands in Dent's main street to commemorate him.

The Sun Inn

Road to Cowgill, Dent Station & Dalehead

The George & Dragon

Road to Ingleton via Deepdale & Kingsdale

Sedgwick memorial

Main Street

Standing proudly at the top of Dent's cobbled main street for more than 300 years, the Sun Inn is the original Dales village inn. A true pub, unspoilt by modern distractions: no TV, jukebox or fruit machines. Instead, just great value food and drink, an open fire, original coin-studded beams, and good cheer to be had with folks around the bar.

Dent even has its own brewery, one of the most remote in the country. It's in a barn half way up a hillside a couple of miles from the village along a single track road. Outside it's wild Dentdale but inside Dent Brewery is slick and modern. It was founded in 1990 and completely renovated in 2005. In 2006 the brewery bought the George & Dragon in Dent village as its own tap-house, and now supplies award-winning beers to many locations across Yorkshire and the North of England.

23

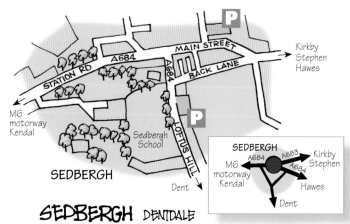

SEDBERGH

SEDBERGH DENTDALE

The east end of Main Street

The west end of Main Street

Like Dent, Sedbergh has been part of Cumbria since 1974. Strung out across the lower slopes of the eastern edges of the Howgill Fells, Sedbergh has the look of a small town and the feel of a large village. It's the furthest west outpost of the Dales National Park, with the Lake District National Park only 18 miles away. Despite a miniscule market place, the narrow main street has a good selection of small town shops and is relieved of heavy through traffic by the Back Lane.

Sedbergh School

Sedbergh has several booksellers along the Main Street and in the wake of the 2001 Foot and Mouth disease outbreak, a project was begun to encourage visitors back to the countryside.

This culminated in 2006 when Sedbergh was officially recognised as "England's Booktown", joining Hay-on-Wye (where the idea started) in Wales and Wigtown in Scotland. The town's secondhand and antiquarian bookshops have been revitalised, and there are various book related festivals throughout the year.

St Andrew's parish church is the town's oldest building by far dating from around 1130. It's part Norman, has an unusual late Victorian stained-glass east window and a chime of eight bells, rung every Sunday.

St Andrew's Church

Sedbergh's biggest claim to fame is its 'public' (that is private and fee-paying) school. It was established in 1525 as a chantry school with scholarships and fellowships to Cambridge University by the Provost of Eton and native of the town, Roger Lupton. It became a free grammar-school in 1552, was rebuilt in 1716, and re-constituted as a public school in 1874. The original 1716 building on the Dent road is now a library and museum.

The school is the town's biggest employer, with its buildings and playing fields covering most of the southern fringes. Boys and girls between the ages of four and eighteen are educated, mainly as boarders. William Wordsworth's son and grandson were pupils and the poet Coleridge taught here until he was sacked for being drunk. More recent alumni include rugby players Will Carling, Will Greenwood and Phil Dowson. Fees can begin at £22,000 a year and – no surprise in such magnificent surroundings – the emphasis is on sport and outdoor activities.

School library & museum

The Main Street at Town Head

The railway arrived here in the 1870s, opening up markets for local stone, agricultural and dairy products, as well as bringing in tourists. Hawes was terminus for the Midland Railway branch line to the Settle to Carlisle Railway and the North Eastern Railway's line from Northallerton. The lines were closed to passengers in 1954 and to freight in 1964.

The old station buildings now house the National Park and Tourist Information centres plus the Dales Countryside Museum, where imaginative displays cover all aspects of life in the Dales and how the landscape has evolved.

HAWES WENSLEYDALE

Prominently located at the head of Wensleydale on the A684, the only main road across the northern dales, Hawes is always busy. It's also at 850ft (260m) above sea level, Yorkshire's highest market town and, with high fells to the north and south, there are spectacular views between the warm-coloured limestone buildings.

Small independent shops line the broad main street, including numerous pubs, hotels and cafés. Popular walking routes abound and the Pennine Way passes through the town. There's a regular market and, generally at the weekends, gatherings of large groups of bikers add spice to the lively and colourful scene.

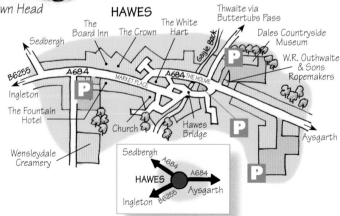

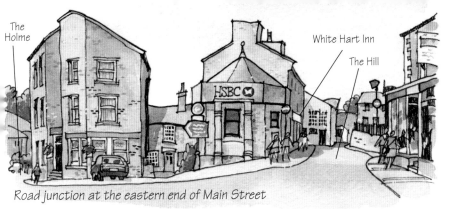

The
Holme

White Hart Inn

The Hill

Road junction at the eastern end of Main Street

The church of St Margaret was built in 1850, its soaring tower, capped by a distinctive pepper-pot spire, dominating the town's skyline. Some of the church pews carry a carved mouse – trademark of the legendary North Yorkshire furniture maker Robert 'Mouseman' Thompson.

After rain there are fine views of Gayle Beck cascading over limestone ledges from Hawes Bridge, a former packhorse bridge at the heart of the old settlement.

Cheese has been made continuously in the dale for over 800 years, following traditional recipes introduced by French monks who settled here in the 12th century. The Wensleydale Creamery Centre in Gayle Lane was established in 1954. In 1966 the Milk Marketing Board bought the factory and in 1992 decided to close it and move production to – horror of horrors – Lancashire! After a huge outcry there was a management buyout and the establishment of today's thriving business. Wensleydale cheese now has a string of celebrity endorsements, including most prominently, the cartoon characters Wallace and Gromit.

W.R. Outhwaite & Sons are one of the last remaining ropemakers in the country, making all manner of products from string to church bell pulls and skipping ropes to carrier bag handles. Their factory on the Aysgarth road is open to the public and well-worth a visit.

The eastern end of Main Street & St Margaret's Church

ASKRIGG WENSLEYDALE

Sitting comfortably at the foot of sheltering fells, the village of Askrigg is dominated by Askrigg Common rising behind it. A minor road between Hawes and Bolton Abbey crosses the northern side of Wensleydale, sweeping through the village. Two scenic roads climb north to cross wild moorland into Swaledale.

Askrigg is little more than a single main street, but is bordered almost continuously by elegant stone houses, giving it the look of a town rather than a small Dales village. There's a pub at each end, a few shops and tea rooms, a 15th-century church and a market cross.

Most of the houses date from the 18th and 19th centuries when Askrigg became a prosperous centre for clock-making, lead-mining and textiles. The Richmond to Lancaster turnpike also came through the village in 1751.

The Crown Inn There has been an inn on this site since the late 18th century

Moorland road into Swaledale

The northern end of Main Street

28

Askrigg became famous through its role as the fictional Darrowby in the hugely popular BBC TV series *All Creatures Great and Small*, which ran for 90 episodes, in two series during 1978-80 and 1988-90. Skeldale House, where exterior scenes of the veterinary surgery were shot, is now bed and breakfast accommodation, while the King's Arms across the street appeared as the Drovers Arms.

The TV series was adapted from the books written by Alf Wright, a vet who actually lived and worked in Thirsk, outside the Dales. He wrote under the pseudonym James Herriot and the area where his stories are set is known as 'Herriot Country' by bus tour companies. The popularity of the books and TV series has drawn many visitors to this part of the Dales, and fans of a certain age still happily splash through the ford on the moorland road between Swaledale and Arkendale, which featured in the title sequence.

The King's Arms

Skeldale House

King's Arms

The southern end of Main Street

The King's Arms was built in 1767 as a coaching inn by John Pratt, a local man who made a fortune as a jockey. He became a racehorse breeder and master of the Askrigg Harriers, keeping his hunters and hounds in a yard behind main street.

The market cross was erected in 1830, almost 250 years after Elizabeth 1 gave the village its charter.

A ring set in the cobbles by the cross dates from the 18th century, when bulls were tethered here to be baited by dogs.

AYSGARTH
Hawes
Edwardian Rock Garden
George and Dragon Inn
Leyburn

Carperby
Falls
Hawes
R Ure
AYSGARTH
A684
Leyburn

Edwardian Rock Garden

AYSGARTH WENSLEYDALE

A village of two parts, Aysgarth straggles for about a mile along the A684 main road through Wensleydale. Apart from a 17th-century coaching inn, the George and Dragon, a few guest houses and a tea room, the western part is largely unremarkable.

However, the Aysgarth Edwardian Rock Garden is worth stopping for. Originally constructed for local man Frank Sayer Graham as his own alpine paradise, it became neglected after his death until being restored by Adrian and Rosemary Anderson and opened to the public in 2003.

The garden is a walk-through grotto of huge water worn limestone blocks rising to about 25ft (8m) in places, low stone lintels and narrow winding paths. A mountain stream and cascade add to the alpine atmosphere and there's a lawned area at the rear. Entry is free but contributions for upkeep are always welcome. Enjoy!

Aysgarth Falls were made famous in Kevin Costner's 1990s film *Robin Hood, Prince of Thieves*, as the setting for Robin's fight with Little John. They are a triple flight of waterfalls extending over a mile-long stretch of the River Ure.

The falls are fast-flowing, especially after wet weather, as thousands of gallons of water cascade over a series of broad limestone steps. Lower Falls have the deepest drop and a viewing platform close to the action.

Yore Mill was built in 1784, one of the earliest examples of 'industrialisation' in a rural setting. Destroyed by a fire in 1852, it was rebuilt at twice the original size and has had various uses since. Corn grinding ended in 1958 and until 1969 it was a cattle food depot. In 2005, the Mill Race Teashop was opened in part of the mill above the river.

St Andrew's church overlooks the mill from its unusually large four-acre churchyard. The site dates from the early 13th century but the church was substantially rebuilt in 1536 and restored in 1866. A number of fittings rescued from Jervaulx Abbey on the Dissolution of the Monasteries are preserved within the church.

The excellent National Park Centre and café has a large car park and is well-placed for walks through the woods, visiting all the falls and the surrounding countryside.

Upper Falls

Yore Mill

Carperby & Castle Bolton

National Park Centre

Middle falls

Upper falls

R Ure

Yore Mill

St Andrew's church

Aysgarth Falls Hotel

The Falls café/bar

Aysgarth village

A684

Leyburn

31

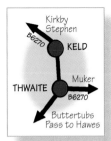

THWAITE
SWALEDALE

Most northerly of the Yorkshire Dales, Swaledale is austerely beautiful. It's narrowness makes it more intimate than the other dales, and with its fabulous patterns of stone walls, a profusion of stone field barns and, in the upper reaches, the abundance of wild flowers in the green fields, Swaledale is many people's favourite.

Centuries of lead mining in the dale have long gone, with nature gradually erasing the scars and remnants of its impact on the landscape. Miner's tracks now invite walkers to explore Swaledale's intimate delights.

Entered over a pretty bridge crossing Straw Beck, Thwaite is little more than a huddle of stone cottages and a red phone box set beneath the smooth slopes of Kisdon and Great Shunner Fell. The buildings aren't pretty but their sturdy shapes and grey-brown sandstone – quarried locally – are in complete harmony with their surroundings. Thwaite was the home and birthplace of the brothers Richard and Cherry Kearton, pioneers in wildlife photography at the end of the 19th century. Their name lives on in the Kearton Tea Rooms and Guesthouse in the centre of the village.

A survey in 1998 counted more than 1,000 field barns in Swaledale, the greatest concentration in the Dales. Most were built between 1750 and 1850 to house livestock in the winter and for storing hay. Solidly built, often two-storey and with stone roofs, they are, along with the field walls, the dominating feature of the Swaledale landscape.

However, many barns – 25% according to the survey – were in a ruinous state or in need of serious repair, but grants have now enabled many derelict barns to be restored. Others have been converted to desirable homes or bunkhouses for walkers.

Thwaite from the B6270 road

Main Street, Keld

KELD SWALEDALE

The narrow road from Thwaite to Keld is a switchback of scenic delights, with the hills gathering in, a barn at every turn and stone walls making ever crazier patterns across the rolling green fields.

Keld is an attractive hamlet of low stone houses gathered around a small square with a large United Reform Church, a chapel and a nearby luxury hotel – Keld Lodge, once a shooting lodge. There's also a camp site and an 'honesty' car park.

But possibly, most remarkable of all in this remote setting, the haunt of sheep and hardy walkers, is that Keld has public toilets!

The River Swale flows through Keld into a wooded limestone gorge, before meandering through some of the finest meadows in England. It's a great place to walk and if you fancy something more challenging Keld is close to halfway on the Coast to Coast Walk and the Pennine Way.

Beyond the village a single road turns westwards into the wilderness of Birkdale Common and the austere grandeur of the high Pennine fells, heading for Kirkby Stephen in Cumbria.

Village store &
tea room

St Mary's
church

The Literary
Institute

The centre of Muker

MUKER SWALEDALE

The largest of the three delightful Upper Swaledale villages (Keld and
Thwaite are the others), Muker enjoys a fabulous location at the foot
of Kisdon, an isolated hill over 1,000ft (305m) high. Straw Beck flows
through the village before joining the River Swale nearby. Hay meadows
behind the village are renowned for their rich variety of flowers and grasses.

Although at one time a centre for lead mining, Muker's main economic
activities these days are sheep farming, woollen clothing and tourism.
Many of the buildings date from the early 19th century mining boom and
some have been adapted for modern business. The old school is now a craft
shop and gallery. You can't miss it – there's a sheep on the roof!

The teashop used to be the vicarage, built in 1680. St Mary's Church,
consecrated in 1580, is one of the few churches built during the reign of
Elizabeth 1, with the tower added at the end of the 18th century.

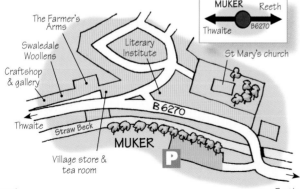

The Farmer's
Arms

Swaledale
Woollens

Craftshop
& gallery

Thwaite

MUKER   Reeth
Thwaite   B6270

Literary
Institute

St Mary's church

B 6270

Straw Beck

MUKER

P

Village store &
tea room

Reeth

The Literary Institute

The Literary Institute dates from 1868 and once housed over 600 books. The ornate, flemish-style building became the practice hall for the Muker Silver Band in 1994. Established to celebrate Queen Victoria's Diamond Jubilee, it's now one of the last surviving bands in Swaledale and Wensleydale, but still maintains a busy calendar of public performances.

The sheep on the Craft Centre roof

In July 2014, TV viewers around the world watched the Tour de France cycle race pass through North Yorkshire. In glorious sunny weather, the Dales looked wonderful. One of the most memorable sights was the cyclists sweeping across this bridge in Muker during the Leeds to Harrogate stage.

35

The north side of the green

REETH
SWALEDALE

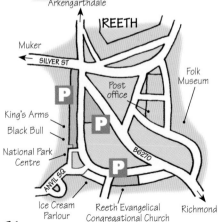

In contrast to other Swaledale villages where buildings seem to huddle together for warmth and protection, Reeth proudly spreads itself around a huge sloping, triangular and partially cobbled green. There's a great sense of space and importance which seems appropriate for Swaledale's largest village and the 18th-century capital of the local lead mining industry. In its heyday Reeth is said to have produced 10% of England's lead.

Situated at the meeting point of the two most northerly Yorkshire Dales, Swaledale and Arkengarthdale, the village is overlooked by the fells of Fremington Edge and Calver Hill. With its open aspect there are fine views all round. It's splendid walking country, particularly along the nearby Arkle Beck.

Large houses around the green testify to Reeth's 18th-century wealth. There are also three fine old inns. The oldest is the Black Bull, dating from 1680. One of its inn signs is hung upside down, a legacy of a dispute over the rendering of the outside walls between a previous landlord and National Park officials.

The King's Arms Hotel, next door, dates back to 1734 and is affectionately called the 'Middle House' by locals due to its position overlooking the green.

With distinctive white walls, the Buck Hotel dominates the top corner of the green. An old coaching inn, it's relatively 'new', dating to around 1760, and once collected tolls from passing travellers.

The south side of the green

Run by volunteers and housed in the old Methodist School Room, used to billet soldiers while training at Catterick Camp during the war, Reeth's Folk Museum contains an eclectic collection of curios illuminating local history and life. Well worth a visit.

Reeth Evangelical Congregational Church stands rather gloomily at the southern end of the green. Grouped with the nearby alleys, chimney pots and gable ends, it has the look an L.S. Lowry painting.

The village attracts many tourists and enjoys all the trappings of a popular Dales tourist hotspot – pretty stone houses, cafés, tearooms, gift shops, a post office – even an ice cream parlour – but Reeth still retains a quiet dignity that's hugely appealing.

The view along Swaledale to Richmond

Malhamdale is one of the shorter dales – about seven miles long – but also one of the most popular, as it packs a lot into its short length. This is premier league limestone country, drawing visitors from around the world to walk amongst some of the most spectacular scenery in the country. They all converge on the small village of Malham, the only place in the upper dale where you can legally park.

Main Street, Malham

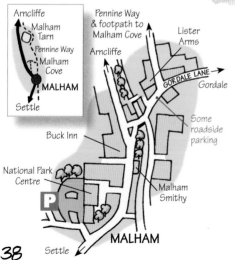

MALHAM MALHAMDALE

Mentioned in the Domesday book as 'Malgun', Malham has been a settlement for at least a thousand years. Traces of Iron age boundaries are still visible today. One hundred years ago, Malham was a place of mills and mines but nowadays hill farming and tourism are the main activities.

A lazy stream, Malham Beck, bisects the village, crossed by a number of clapper bridges and a much-photographed packhorse bridge at the centre. Low stone cottages, many dating back to the 18th century, peep from behind trees adding a pleasingly sylvan flavour to the characteristic Dales harmony.

Most of the time Malham has the air of a laid-back, quiet village. It's usually busy but in high season it's crazy! Two pubs and a scattering of shops and cafés cope valiantly with the legions of visitors, here for the numerous walks, taking a break from walking the Pennine Way or just wandering around the village.

The National Park Centre is a particularly good one but the large car park attached to it soon fills up, so get there early.

The Buck Inn was built in 1874 on the site of an old coaching inn. Now a popular eatery, famous for its Malham & Masham Pies which are made on the premises from chunks of locally reared beef steak and Old Peculiar gravy. At busy times more than 500 of them are sold.

On the other side of the packhorse bridge there's a small green which you can park alongside – if you're lucky. Facing it is The Lister Arms, a traditional coaching inn with the date of 1723 over the door, many period features, climbing ivy on the outside wall and a mounting block for riders to climb aboard their horses.

Tilly

Malham Smithy

The Malham Smithy was bequeathed to the Parish Church by artist and village blacksmith Bill Wild in the early 1980's. Since then it has been leased as a traditional blacksmith's workshop.

In February 2007, Annabelle Bradley made the life-changing move from tax accountant to blacksmith. She now helps to keep this vital part of Dales village heritage alive, producing all manner of forged artifacts from sculptural pieces to novelty bottle openers. Annabelle is 'helped' by her labrador dog, Tilly, who likes to sleep in the doorway. You may have to step over her to enter the smithy.

Malham village has a lot going for it but really it's only the waiting room for the main event – Malham Cove.

The Lister Arms

The packhorse bridge & Malham Beck

MALHAM COVE MALHAMDALE

One of the great wonders of the Yorkshire Dales, Malham Cove is a curved limestone cliff 262ft (80m) high and 984ft (300m) wide. You have to stand beneath it to appreciate the scale of this natural amphitheatre.

An easy walk off the minor road to Ayscliffe guides you along the beckside to the foot of the Cove. An alternative route is the Pennine Way out of Malham along the lane beside the Lister Arms. This climbs steeply up the western side of the Cove, then crosses onto a wide limestone pavement with clints (small flat blocks) and grikes (deep crevices between). These were created by rainwater slowly seeping through the rock after melting glaciers scoured it clean some 50,000 years ago. The pavement requires care to walk on but it's an awesome viewpoint.

Originally a large waterfall plunged over the Cove. This outflow from Malham Tarn now disappears underground and was assumed to be the source of Malham Beck, which flows from the Cove base. However, tests with dyes have disproved this and suggested a possible complex of caves behind the cliff. Potholers have so far explored around a mile of passages.

Although the minor road to Ayscliffe passes close to the Cove as it climbs out of the village, there's strictly no parking at the roadside. You have to park in the village and walk. It's always worth it.

Scenes for *Harry Potter and The Deathly Hallows* were filmed around Malham, including Malham Cove, the limestone pavement, Malham Tarn and Gordale Scar.

Gordale Scar is a spectacular gorge between high limestone cliffs just east of Malham. Leave the village on Gardale Lane and have a look at Janet's Foss, a pretty waterfall, then take a well-signed footpath opposite to the Scar. Continue through the canyon to the waterfall at the end, which hardy walkers climb on a popular seven-mile route taking in all three of Malham's limestone spectaculars. Yes, they generally do get wet!

Malhamdale from the Ayscliffe road

Malham Tarn

Malham Tarn lies 1,237ft (377m) above sea level, the highest lake in England. It's claimed to be the inspiration for Charles Kingsley's 1863 novel, *The Water Babies*. You can walk to the Tarn from the Cove following a well-trodden route via Ing Scar and Comb Hill.

Driving to it is difficult but you can park at Watersinks car park, which is nearby. This is accessed about three miles out of Malham on the Ayscliffe road, turning right onto an unsigned road with the Tarn in sight ahead and passing Low Trenhouse farm.

The road bridge over Kettlewell Beck and the Blue Bell Inn

KETTLEWELL WHARFEDALE

Wharfedale is one of Yorkshire's great river valleys. From its source in the wilds of Langstrothdale the River Wharfe flows south through Kettlewell, Grassington and Burnsall, eventually joining the Ouse at Cawood. The upper reaches are most attractive with Kettlewell, the largest village and furthest north, beautifully situated at the junction with lonely but beautiful Coverdale.

A weekly corn market brought some prosperity to the village during the 13th century and it has a history of lead mining. But like many of the pretty Yorkshire villages, Kettlewell's survival now relies on farming, tourism, holiday homes and commuters.

Visitors are well catered for, as Kettlewell boasts three inns, numerous guest houses and B&Bs, a village store and, in the large car park by the river, an old-fashioned garage with pumps – the only fuel supplier between Grassington and Aysgarth.

The inns all provide accommodation and serve meals. Two of them face each other near the main bridge. The Blue Bell and the Racehorses are now both comfortable traditional village hostelries despite the Racehorses once being the Blue Bell's stables. There's another pub at the eastern end of the village, the King's Head, another family-run establishment with a number of awards to its name.

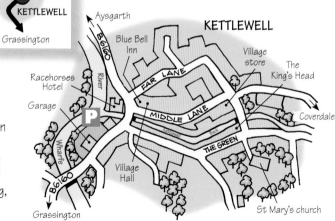

The village store

Bisected by Kettlewell Beck, the village's squat stone buildings, crowded together in a seemingly haphazard way, are a delightful chaos of narrow roads, footbridges, alleys, yards and pretty walled gardens.

This provided the idyllic setting for the 2003 film *Calendar Girls*, based on the true story of members of a Yorkshire Women's Institute who posed nude for a calendar to raise funds for a local hospital. The actual calendar girls came from Cracoe and Rylstone, villages near Grassington.

The main road touches only the western side of the village and a stroll around the quiet lanes reveals a number of 17th- and 18th-century houses, including the vicarage. The church is a Victorian rebuild on a medieval site.

Kettlewell is on the Dales Way and is a popular starting point for ascents of Great Whernside and Buckden Pike. Rights of way connect the village to Nidderdale and Arncliffe in Littondale.

KILNSEY CRAG WHARFEDALE

Three miles south of Kettlewell, the hamlet of Kilnsey is pleasant enough, with a handful of houses, the Tennant Arms Hotel and a popular trout farm, but it's the nearby crag which grabs the attention. Created by glacial action during the Ice Age, the gigantic wall of Great Scar Limestone rises dramatically 170ft (52m) above the B6160 road. Near the top there's a 40ft (12m) overhang, an irresistible challenge for climbers, who are regularly seen clinging precariously to the rock.

LINTON WHARFEDALE

First sight of Linton can be a huge and pleasant surprise. Set in attractive open farmland on the west side of the valley, with the River Wharfe separating it from Grassington, the tiny village is secluded within a great wall of trees. It's Wharfedale's hidden gem.

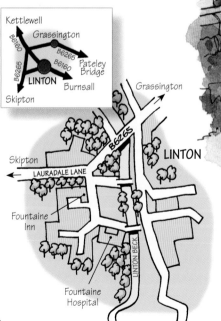

The 14th century packhorse bridge and the Fountaine Inn

At the heart of the village groups of 17th- and 18th-century grey-stone houses stand informally around a large sloping green. Linton Beck flows along the bottom edge, crossed by a clapper bridge, a packhorse bridge and a modern road bridge. Various fords, stepping stones, and huge and verdant trees complete the picturesque scene.

White-walled Fountaine Inn sits at the top of the green, a perfect spot to sit and watch lines of ducks waddle across the grass. There's no car park in this part of Linton but roadside parking – with consideration – is permitted.

Linton's agreeable air of peace and dignity is partly due to the dominating presence of Fountaine Hospital, Wharfedale's grandest building, thought to have been designed by Sir John Vanbrugh. The almshouse was built in 1721 to provide accommodation for poor men and women of the parish. Run by trustees, the charity still operates and a chapel at the centre of the building is open to the public. It was bequeathed by Richard Fountaine, an undertaker who made his fortune in London during the Plague of 1665 and the Great Fire a year later.

St Michael's Church, by the River Wharfe a half mile from the main village, dates from the late 12th century. It has much of interest and is said to be the oldest church still in regular use in the country. There's a small car park in the lane to the church, a good place to stop for a stroll to admire the Linton Falls on the Wharfe. Nearby are some much-photographed stepping-stones across the broad river.

Linton Beck and clapper bridge

Fountaine Hospital 45

GRASSINGTON WHARFEDALE

Wharfedale's largest settlement, Grassington feels to the casual visitor like a village but it has long held the status of a town, being granted a market and fair charter in 1282. Situated at the crossing of two important highways, the B6160 Ilkley to Aysgarth road and the B6265 Pately Bridge to Skipton, Grassington is generally regarded as the capital of Upper Wharfedale.

Lead mining brought some prosperity in the 17th century but the next two centuries were the town's boom time with important mining developments on Grassington Moor, the arrival of turnpike roads and the growth of the local textile industry in watermills along the river. The opening of the Yorkshire Dales Railway to nearby Threshfield in 1901 brought new visitors. As the industry declined the number of tourists began to increase and has never abated since.

Church House
17th century yeoman's farmhouse

The Pump

Grassington House
Luxury hotel in Georgian building

Upper Wharfedale Folk Museum

The Square

The Black Horse Hotel
17th-century coaching inn

Garrs Lane at the top of the Square

Church House
A place of worship for Grassington people as the Parish Church is some distance away across the River Wharfe

Supplied the village with water during the 19th century

The Pump

A cobbled yard of 17th century stone cottages leading off the top end of Main Street. A large house at the end of the yard is thought to have been the town courtroom – hence the name

Chamber End Fold

Grassington's village atmosphere is mainly due to most of the tourist 'attractions' being concentrated around the cobbled square at its centre. In and around it are four pubs and a good range of food, clothes and gift shops plus various eateries, quaint stone cottages and colourful gardens. A hour or two exploring Grassington's narrow streets and numerous alleys is never time wasted.

47

Burnsall, the River Wharfe and the road bridge

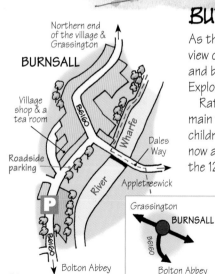

BURNSALL

Northern end of the village & Grassington

Village shop & a tea room

Roadside parking

Wharfe

Dales Way

River

Appletreewick

B6160

P

B6160

Bolton Abbey

Grassington

BURNSALL

B6160

Bolton Abbey

BURNSALL WHARFEDALE

As the B6160 road from Bolton Abbey dips across the lower slopes of Burnsall Fell, a memorable view of Burnsall appears, with the meandering River Wharfe, the elegant bridge, brownstone buildings and background hills climbing to dark moorland, all combining for a perfect picture of rural harmony. Exploring the village itself is no less of a treat.

Rather oddly Burnsall village is split into two parts with a couple of fields separating them. The main tourist area is well organised with a village shop, tearoom, large car park and grassy areas for children to play on along the riverside. The Red Lion Hotel, originally a 16th-century ferryman's inn, is now a fine place to sit outside and watch the world go by. The cellars of the inn are said to date from the 12th century and to be haunted by a poltergeist.

The blissful scene is dominated by the broad, free-flowing River Wharfe, complete with various noisy wildfowl and the handsome five-arched road bridge, built in 1884, sweeping across it. The Green on the eastern side of the river is a closely-mown cricket field. With Burnsall Fell as background and the river encircling half its boundary, it could be considered as one of the most scenic pitches in England. Sadly though, it appears to host no regular cricket matches and there's no permanent pavilion, although special events are held here.

48

A 17th-century schoolroom in the northern part of the village resembles a small manor house with a two-storied gabled porch and mullioned windows. It was founded in 1602 by Sir William Craven, 'The Dick Whittington of the Dales', who was born at nearby Appletreewick and rose from poverty to become Lord Mayor of London between 1610 and 1612. He returned to the Dales and lavished his wealth on local projects such as the improvement of the church and the then bridge, and the endowment of the school, which is still used to educate primary school children.

Sir William has a commemorative plaque in the nearby ancient church of St Wilfred, which has a pretty lych-gate and some hog-back gravestones thought to date from the 10th century. The main building is perpendicular in style, largely 13th century, though the font is from the 11th.

Burnsall's mellow stone buildings date from the 18th and 19th centuries, many with mullioned windows. With its splendid setting and beautifully kept green areas, the village is a popular setting for weddings and corporate events. Burnsall Fell, the route for annual fell races to its 1,661ft (506m) summit, overlooks the blissful scene like a doting grandparent.

A Burnsall doorway

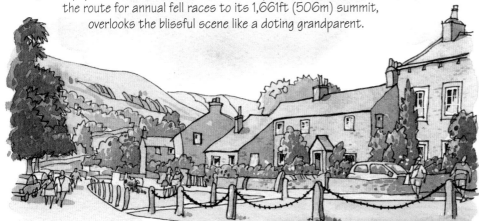

Cottages, the shop and tearoom overlooking the river

The Dales Way, a 76-mile long-distance walk, mainly through the Dales National Park, runs from Ilkley in Yorkshire to the shores of Windermere in Cumbria, and follows the River Wharfe through Wharfedale. For an excellent circular walk around Burnsall village, join the Dales Way on the riverbank near the Red Lion, walk upstream to the northern end of the village and return along the road. It's flat, easy walking and you'll see all that's best about this lovely place.

49

LITTONDALE

It was Vendale for Charles Kingsley, Amerdale for William Wordsworth and ITV chose it as the setting for *Emmerdale Farm*, but to connoisseurs of secluded and stirring limestone country it has always been Littondale.

The drive from Malham is fabulous, from farmland beyond Malham Tarn to open moorland with great fell views and the lonely farmstead of Darnbrook House. Here a sharp right turn and a steep climb onto Nab End takes you to an elevated unfenced road with an awesome view of the dramatic limestone contours of Yew Cogar Scar, almost two miles long, towering over Cowside Beck. The winding descent past limestone walls and barns to the green fields of Litterdale is equally memorable.

The Falcon Inn and Arncliffe green

An Arncliffe cottage

Arncliffe is a pretty Dales village with an ancient church and a nearby bridge of similar age which leads to a long, narrow green surrounded by low, solidly-built stone cottages and farms.

The Falcon Inn occupies the far corner of the green, a proudly, old-fashioned hostelry which starred as the original Woolpack in *Emmerdale Farm* when the TV soap opera began in 1972. It serves hearty food and real ale and is the perfect place to refuel after enjoying a walk along the river or across the hills.

The Queen's Arms, Litton

Halton Gill

Littondale has been inhabited since the Iron Age. In Norman times it was a hunting forest and later a medieval sheep-rearing estate of Fountains Abbey. The farming pattern has changed little since — sheep on the hills and cattle in the riverside meadows. Littondale has the distinction of being one of the few Yorkshire Dales not scarred by lead mining. The small linear settlements along the river have chunky limestone houses and cottages with dark, low pitched roofs.

Most of the magnificent barns, many with covered porches, date from the time when corn was grown. Some have been converted to desirable homes, especially at Halton Gill, a cluster of mainly 17th-century farms and cottages at the foot of Horse Head Pass, an old packhorse route into Langstrothdale.

The Queen's Arms at Littondale is an attractive little inn serving food. When pubs in more populous areas of the country are reportably closing at an alarming rate, it's heartening to find a thriving one in such a relatively remote place.

Litton

51

DALES MOTOR TOURS

The Hawes Round. Approx 40 miles
Swaledale, Wensleydale, Buttertubs Pass and Bolton Castle

At the eastern end of Hawes take the road signed 'Muker' and climb to the 1,726ft (526m) summit of Buttertubs Pass, a tough test for Tour de France cyclists in 2014. Look out for the famous buttertubs, a series of limestone swallow-holes where Swaledale farmers returning from Hawes market were said to store their unsold butter.

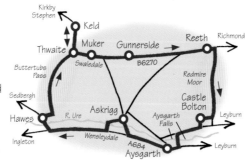

Visit Thwaite (p32) and take the narrow walled road to Keld (p33) through classic Swaledale countryside. Return down the dale to Muker (p34) and Reeth (p36).

Just beyond Reeth leave the B6270 onto a minor road signed 'Redmire' and climb steeply to Redmire Moor for more superlative views. Descend to Castle Bolton, a tranquil village of stone cottages set around a green with a magnificent castle at the end. Built in 1399, the structure is remarkably complete with over a third of the rooms still intact. Mary, Queen of Scots, was detained here in 1568 and the castle has been a setting for many films. A minor road takes you directly to Aysgarth Falls (p30), from where you take the A684 through Wensleydale back to Hawes (p26), with a short detour to visit Askrigg (p28).

The Skipton Round. Approx 45 miles
Malhamdale, Littondale, and 'Calendar Girls Country'

Leave Skipton on the A65 and take a minor road north to Malham (p38). Beyond the village climb for good views of Malham Cove (p40) and Malham Tarn, before crossing Malham Moor and descending into Littondale (p50). Drive down the dale for a short diversion on the B6160 to Kettlewell (p42).

Return south, following the River Wharfe to Linton (p44), Grassington (p46) and Burnsall (p48). Continue on the B6160 to perhaps visit Bolton Abbey estate; 30,000 acres of wonderful countryside with over 80 miles of footpaths and the famous ruins of Bolton Priory. The A59 returns you to Skipton.

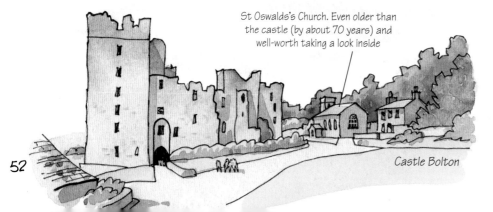

St Oswalds's Church. Even older than the castle (by about 70 years) and well-worth taking a look inside

Castle Bolton

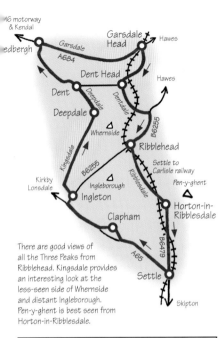

There are good views of all the Three Peaks from Ribblehead. Kingsdale provides an interesting look at the less-seen side of Whernside and distant Ingleborough. Pen-y-ghent is best seen from Horton-in-Ribblesdale.

PLEASE NOTE

Parts of all three of these routes are on narrow moorland roads. Though perfectly safe to drive on in dry weather, these exposed routes can become dangerous in rain and mist. To drive on them in wintery conditions would be extremely foolish.

However, these remote areas are hugely attractive, so if the weather is favourable head for the moorland uplands. The breathtaking views will live with you forever.

The Settle Round. Approx 60 miles

Kingsdale, Deepdale, Dentdale, Garsdale Ribblesdale & the Three Peaks

Take the A65 west from Settle and the short diversion to Clapham (p10). Return to the main road and continue to Ingleton (p12). Take the road past the Ingleton Waterfalls Trust out of the village and follow the signs to 'Dent'.

At the Marton Arms in Thornton in Longsdale, turn sharp right onto a minor road which climbs to nine miles of lonely moorland and fellside before dropping down to the green fields of Deepdale and the village of Dent (p22). Continue to Sedbergh (p24) then along the A684 to Garsdale Head, a remote huddle of railway workers houses set amongst rolling fells. Turn right, climbing up a single track road (with passing places) to high moorland with sensational views.

Descend past Dent station, another lonely railway outpost, and turn left up Dentdale (p20), following the river and railway. Pass Artengill Viaduct and go under Dent Head Viaduct as the road climbs out of the dale. Join the B6255 and follow the crowds to the iconic Ribblehead Viaduct at Ribblehead (p16).

Continue to follow the railway through Horton in Ribblesdale (p14) and back to Settle (p8).

High Street

SKIPTON

The 'Gateway to the Dales', as Skipton bills itself, is just that, the perfect base for exploring the Dales. The small town sits handily on the southern edge of the National Park with the A65 west to Cumbria providing easy access to minor roads heading north.

Skipton is a friendly, interesting place with one of England's best-preserved medieval castles and a church of similar vintage. Lively market stalls line the award-winning high street four times a week. Characterful alleyways and squares link the many excellent shops, pubs and restaurants.

The town is also at the intersection of the trans-Pennine Leeds and Liverpool Canal (opened in 1770) and the Springs Canal, built soon after to transport limestone. A statue of professional Yorkshireman and cricketer 'Fiery' Freddie Truman in fearsome mid-bowling flight stands on the canal wharf.

53

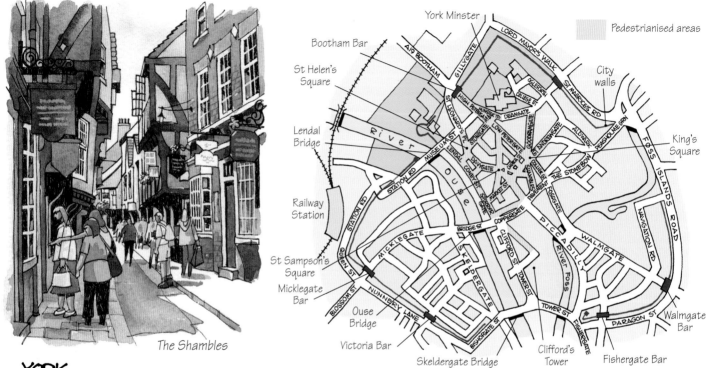

The Shambles

Pedestrianised areas

York Minster
Bootham Bar
St Helen's Square
Lendal Bridge
Railway Station
St Sampson's Square
Micklegate Bar
Ouse Bridge
Victoria Bar
Skeldergate Bridge
Clifford's Tower
Fishergate Bar
Walmgate Bar
King's Square
City walls

YORK

Now a world-famous tourist attraction with more than four million visitors a year, York has the X factor that manufactured theme parks cannot match. It's called history and goes back 2000 years. The Romans, Anglo-Saxons, Vikings and Normans all settled here, each leaving a legacy that's still enjoyed today.

Modern York effortlessly combines its rich heritage with being a totally 21st-century city. It's compact size and traffic-free centre make it perfect for exploring on foot. Small it may be, but you'll find high-end shops and boutiques, chic restaurants, atmospheric pubs and smart cafés. Museums abound and there's a vibrant culture of film, theatre and music.

And of course there's the Minster, the largest Gothic Cathedral in Northern Europe, a masterpiece of medieval architecture. You can't get better than that.

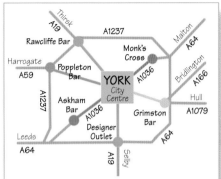

York's park & ride sites

York has numerous car parks but the best way for motorists to visit the city is to use the excellent park and ride system.

There are six parks around the perimeter, so from whatever direction you approach there'll be a convenient one near you. The car parks are large and buses run frequently into the city centre.

York's train station is handily placed just outside the city walls and open-topped tour buses will take you to all the main attractions in comfort.

York's wealth and fame has been aided by that most enduring of comfort foods – chocolate. For over 300 years, the Rowntree, Terry and Craven families made York world-famous for its chocolates and sweets. In 1939 their local factories employed over 12,000 people.

The Rowntree family were influential social reformers, pioneering many improvements in factory conditions, and the Terry family played a prominent part in York's civic affairs, with Joseph Terry elected four times as Lord Mayor.

Today's confectionery business isn't as vibrant as it was but six million Kit Kat bars are still produced in York every day – over one billion a year.

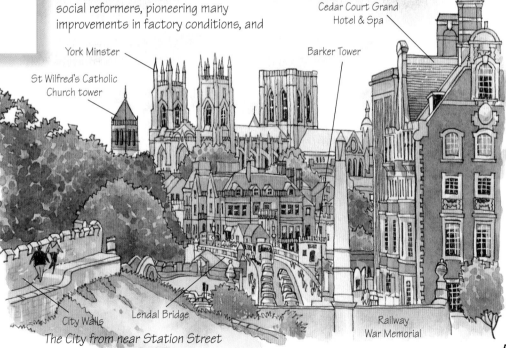

The City from near Station Street

York has the longest medieval town walls in England. Though built by the Romans and restored by the Danes, most of what survives is actually from the 12th to 14th centuries. They are in remarkably good condition and feature five main bars (or gateways), a Victorian gateway, a postern (back or side entrance) and 45 towers.

Walking a complete circuit of the walls, around two miles, is a great way to get an overall picture of the city. An apparently missing section alongside the Fosse was marshy ground and thought sufficient to deter invaders without a wall.

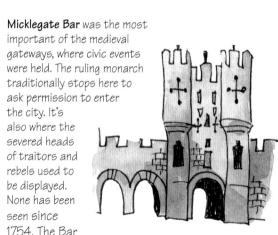

Walmgate Bar

Bootham Bar

Bootham Bar is on the site of the Roman north-west gate. From here Roman Legions marched north to attack Scotland. The three stone statues on the top were added in 1894 and represent a medieval mayor, a knight and a mason who holds a model of the Bar.

Monk Bar is the tallest of the main four gates and a formidable fortress on its own. It was built in the 13th century and still has its original portcullis in working order. Some of the stone figures on the top of the Bar appear to be throwing stones into the street.

Monk Bar

Walmgate Bar still bears the cannonball and bullet scars of the Civil War in 1644 when the combined Parliamentary and Scottish forces besieged the city after York declared its support for the King. An Elizabethan house, supported by stone pillars, clings to the inner side.

Micklegate Bar was the most important of the medieval gateways, where civic events were held. The ruling monarch traditionally stops here to ask permission to enter the city. It's also where the severed heads of traitors and rebels used to be displayed. None has been seen since 1754. The Bar is now a museum.

Micklegate Bar

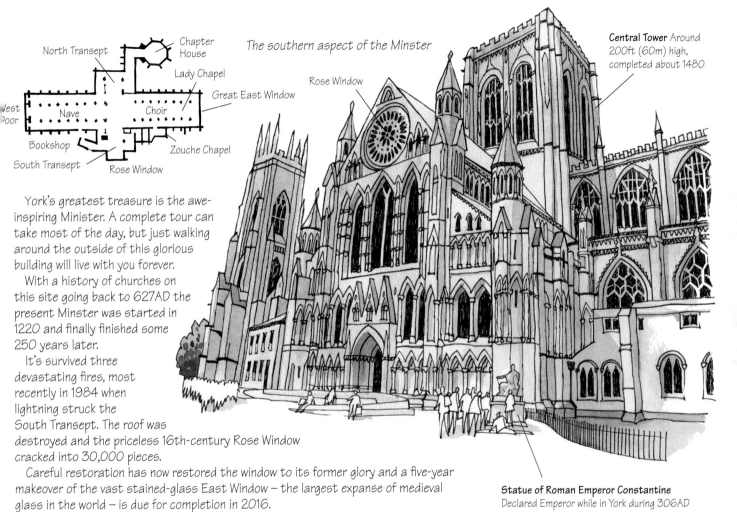

North Transept

Chapter House

Lady Chapel

Great East Window

West Door

Nave

Choir

Bookshop

Zouche Chapel

South Transept

Rose Window

The southern aspect of the Minster

Rose Window

Central Tower Around 200ft (60m) high, completed about 1480

York's greatest treasure is the awe-inspiring Minister. A complete tour can take most of the day, but just walking around the outside of this glorious building will live with you forever.

With a history of churches on this site going back to 627AD the present Minster was started in 1220 and finally finished some 250 years later.

It's survived three devastating fires, most recently in 1984 when lightning struck the South Transept. The roof was destroyed and the priceless 16th-century Rose Window cracked into 30,000 pieces.

Careful restoration has now restored the window to its former glory and a five-year makeover of the vast stained-glass East Window – the largest expanse of medieval glass in the world – is due for completion in 2016.

Statue of Roman Emperor Constantine
Declared Emperor while in York during 306AD

Central York is a fascinating spider's web of tangled alleys and narrow thoroughfares linking the three main squares and open spaces.

Now largely traffic-free, it's a wonderful area to wander around and perhaps turn down some of the 'snickelways' just to see where they lead. Exploring them can open up a vivid mixture of past and present far more evocative than any organised tour.

A quiet day in Stonegate

York's central pedestrianised area is its tourist hotspot. But despite the crowds, it's still a good place to shop, with many upmarket brands and a credible lack of tourist tat.

The Shambles is one of Europe's best-preserved medieval shopping streets. Originally the street of butchers and slaughterhouses, the buildings are positioned close together to keep out the sun. Close enough it's often said, to be able to shake hands across the street from the upstairs windows.

After the Shambles, Stonegate is probably York's second most famous street. It links Minster Gates to St Helen's Square and has been a street for almost 2,000 years, with buildings and architecture of every period from the Normans to the Victorians. A rare beam sign of The Olde Starre Inn dominates the street.

Minster Gates and the west door

The Mansion House, Corey Street

Of the city's three main squares, St Helen's is the most interesting. It was originally the graveyard of St Helen's Church which was cleared in 1745 because, it's said, the number of bodies buried there had created a small hill that made it difficult for carriages to pass.

Dominating the square is one of York's finest Georgian buildings, the Mansion House, completed in 1732. Richly furnished inside, it's the official residence of the Lord Mayor during his term of office. Set in the pavement outside are cobbles marking the line of the old wall and the site of the Praetorian Gate, main entrance into the Roman city.

In stark contrast, St Helen's Church solemnly faces the gaily-coloured Mansion House from across the square. Originally 14th century, it was largely rebuilt in the 16th after a Private Act from Queen Mary stopped its demolition. Now it's York's Civic Church where the Lord Mayor and Corporation attend Harvest Thanksgiving each year.

In 1936 the founder of Betty's, Frederick Belmont, travelled on the maiden voyage of the Queen Mary.

Enthralled by the splendour of the ship, he commissioned the Queen Mary's designers and craftsmen to turn a dilapidated furniture store in St Helen's Square into an elegant café.

A visit to Betty's Tea Shop, surrounded by huge curved windows, elegant wood panelling and ornate mirrors is an essential part of the York visitor experience.

Another local institution began in a fine building nearby. Currently a bar, it was the original headquarters of the Yorkshire Insurance Company. Its name in black letters is still prominent across the front.

Yorkshire Insurance building

St Helen's Church

59

York has a dazzling array of attractions but often it's the little things, the oddities, that add so much flavour to a visit. A huge clock which hangs low over Coney Street outside St Martin-Le-Grand Church would be a serious hazard for double-decker buses if they were allowed in the street. There's a figure on top of the ornate clock holding a cross staff, an early form of sextant, which is known as the 'Little Admiral'. During a World War II air raid In 1942, fire gutted the church and the clock was badly damaged. The 15th-century tower of the church and the 14th-century south aisle have been restored' and the rest of the building converted to a paved garden as a war memorial. The clock, which dates from 1668, and the Little Admiral, first added in 1778, were returned to good health in 1966.

Look out for the printer's devil at the entrance to Coffee Yard, off Stonegate. It identifies a former printer's shop, one of the many that flourished in the city for many years.

Clifford's Tower has been imaginatively called 'York's leaning tower' and perches rather uncertainly on a grassy mound, once surrounded by a moat fed by the River Foss. It's all that remains of York's 13th-century castle, whose turbulent history lasted some 600 years before it was taken under the protective wing of English Heritage. Steep steps up the mound and a spiral staircase take you up to the battlements, from where there's a terrific view over the city. The name is a legacy of one Roger de Clifford whose body hung from the tower in chains after he was found guilty of treason in 1322.

The street name plate of Whip-ma-whop-ma-gate can be found near the Shambles. Even though there's no gate or street to speak of, it has become a kind of tourist attraction as the 'shortest street with the longest name'. Its derivation is uncertain, though most probably it comes from the public floggings that took place on nearby Pavement.

Clifford's Tower, Tower Street

The Ouse riverside and the Lendal Bridge

York lies at the confluence of two major rivers, the Ouse and the Foss, so it's hardly surprising that it sometimes floods. A lovely riverside inn, The King's Arms, has become famous as 'the pub that floods'. A board inside records the height of the floodwater. The worst (so far) was November 2000 when water almost reached the first floor windows.

Most of the time though the river is yet another of York's abundant assets, slicing majestically and picturesquely through the city. It was a busy waterway in medieval times when York was an important port, and products such as wool and lead were transported on boats to Hull for export to Europe. Warehouses along the river have been turned into flats or hotels.

After exploring this vibrant city it's good to relax, maybe on a river cruise, sampling Betty's famous tearooms or eating heartily in the Tudor splendor of Gert & Henry's Restaurant, tucked away behind the market .

Gert & Henry's Restaurant

61

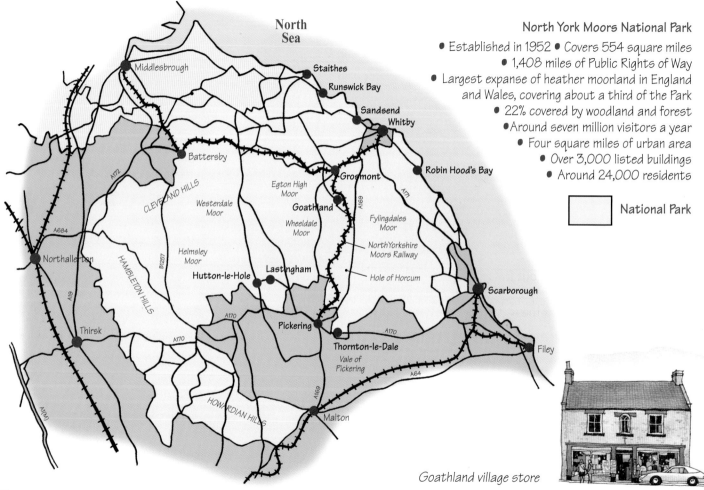

North Sea

Middlesbrough

Staithes

Runswick Bay

Sandsend

Whitby

Battersby

CLEVELAND HILLS

Egton High Moor

Grosmont

Robin Hood's Bay

Westerdale Moor

Goathland

Wheeldale Moor

Fylingdales Moor

A169

A171

Helmsley Moor

North Yorkshire Moors Railway

HAMBLETON HILLS

Hutton-le-Hole

Lastingham

Hole of Horcum

Northallerton

A684

B1257

A172

A19

Thirsk

Scarborough

Pickering

Thornton-le-Dale

A170

A170

Filey

Vale of Pickering

A169

A64

HOWARDIAN HILLS

A1(M)

Malton

North York Moors National Park

- Established in 1952 • Covers 554 square miles
- 1,408 miles of Public Rights of Way
- Largest expanse of heather moorland in England and Wales, covering about a third of the Park
- 22% covered by woodland and forest
- Around seven million visitors a year
- Four square miles of urban area
- Over 3,000 listed buildings
- Around 24,000 residents

National Park

Goathland village store

62

NORTH YORK MOORS NATIONAL PARK

It's Britains's eighth-largest national park and England's largest site of Special Scientific Interest and, despite the name, it's not just moors; there's also 26 miles of spectacular coastline, peaceful valleys, picturesque villages, ancient woods and important historical sites.

The North Yorkshire Moors National Park stretches west almost to Thirsk and south to the Howardian Hills near Malton, but here we concentrate on the main tourist areas along the coastline, the picturesque villages around Pickering and the wonderful North Yorkshire Moors Railway, which winds north through spectacular scenery to Goathland, famous for its starring role in the TV series, *Heartbeat*.

The coastline is stunning but fragile, with cliffs crumbling into the vicious North Sea. Substantial seawalls have been built to prevent the seaside gems of Robin Hood's Bay and Runswick Bay being swept away.

Whitby and Scarborough, North Yorkshire's great tourist warhorses, differ in character but attract huge crowds for their spectacle, history and seaside attractions.

The moors themselves remain great unspoilt wonderlands, populated mainly by sheep but criss-crossed by paths, tracks and minor roads, so are accessible to all. Attractively austere for most of the year, the breezy plateaus become a blaze of dazzling purple when the heather blossoms for a few short weeks in early summer.

As one of England's most beautiful and largest areas of open countryside, the Moors attract anyone who likes to be outdoors, whether it's to drive, walk, cycle, build sand castles or just to sit outside a county pub enjoying the Yorkshire sunshine. Yes it does happen – and being Yorkshire, there's lots of it!

The Moors in glorious purple

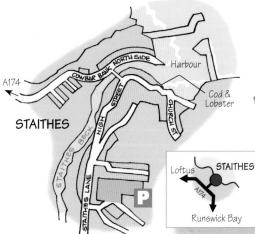

The top of High Street

STAITHES

Hidden away in a deep gorge and sheltered from North Sea storms by the high cliffs of Cowbar Nab and Penny Steel, Staithes is a higgledy-piggledy assortment of closely-packed stone houses, narrow streets and alleys. One of the streets, Dog Loup, is only 18in (48cm) wide, said to be the narrowest in the north.

Once one of the largest fishing ports in England, Staithes still has the air of a rough and ready working village. It was also involved in building boats, making sails, and — aided by its isolation — smuggling. This lack of accessibility is emphasised these days by visitors being banned from driving into the village. You have to park at the top of a hill and walk down a hill, so steep there are seats every so often to rest. Once down into the cramped streets you understand the car ban. There'd be gridlock right away. With hardly enough room for the houses and people, gardens are a luxury.

The Cod & Lobster

Roxy Beck edges the main village, littered by boats and crossed by a footbridge. Though undoubtably quaint and picturesque, Staithes isn't known for its prettiness. But there's a good range of independent shops and eating places plus a homely pub, the Cod and Lobster, right on the sea's edge.

Staithes backstreet

When a young man, James Cook worked in a Staithes grocery shop before moving to Whitby and world fame as explorer, navigator, cartographer, and captain in the Royal Navy.

Apart from fishing, which survives, jet, alum and potash were mined here. Extraction continues at the Boulby Potash Mine, near Staithes, one of the deepest in the United Kingdom. A railway line to Whitby bolstered the industry and a viaduct crossed the gorge, which must have been scary in a North Sea gale. The line closed in 1960 and the viaduct was dismantled.

One of the most admired views in North Yorkshire can be seen by crossing the footbridge and climbing the hill to Cowbar Bank.

Staithes triumphantly succeeds as a tourist attraction by not being 'touristy'. No visitor to the North Yorkshire coast should miss this unspoilt gem.

The classic view from Cowbar Bank

RUNSWICK BAY

Royal Hotel

BANK TOP LANE

A174
Staithes to
Sandsend road

P

P

RUNSWICK
BAY

The view from the top car park

A small community but perfectly formed, Runswick Bay is a delightful fishing village of dinky, red-roofed houses cascading down a cleft in the cliffs. A rocky headland sweeps around the bay like a protecting arm. Multi-coloured pebbles spatter the beach, evidence of the many minerals — jet, alum, iron and potash — once mined here.

A steep hill descends from Bank Top Lane to a large car park by the beach. First sight of the bay from the hilltop on a sunny day can be breathtaking, and rates highly on the WOW-factor scale.

The village is split into two parts with the houses at the top being made to look ordinary by the dazzling display going on below. There's a car park at the top and the Royal Hotel, a friendly pub, family-run for over 15 years, with idyllic views across the bay.

Scenes around the village

The bottom part of the village has a variety of treats. Apart from the pretty houses and gardens climbing up the wooded cliff, there's an ancient thatched coastguard's cottage, a lifeboat house and a tiny café selling homemade cakes and pastries.

The village has suffered storm damage and was rebuilt in the 17th century after a landslide destroyed the old one. A seawall was built in 1970.

With scenic paths heading both North and South on the Cleveland Way, Runswick Bay has everything the discerning visitor needs.

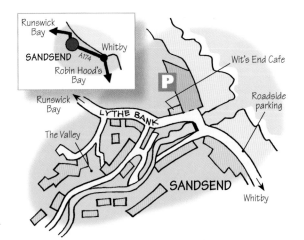

SANDSEND

With deference to Yorkshire's reputation for plain-speaking, Sandsend is exactly that. It's where the almost three miles stretch of sand between West Pier, Whitby and Sandsend Ness ends.

At first sight it's a proper seaside village with a fine beach and the requisite pubs, gift shops and cafés lined up along the beachside road. The Wits End Café is over 100 years old and has a walled garden, free car parking and a fine sea view across Sandsend Bay to Whitby.

Just yards inland, however, lies the most delightful little village of red-roofed cottages with a river meandering through a patchwork of greens. There's winding pathways, little wooden bridges, tree-lined hillsides and colourful gardens straight out of an estate agent's dream world. Indeed that's exactly what it is, as property prices here are said to be the highest on the Yorkshire coast.

Sandsend beach and Whitby

The Valley, as this part of Sandsend is aptly called, occupies a large portion of the western side of the village and is part of the 16,000-acre Mulgrave Estate, considered to be one of England's finest shooting grounds. The estate boasts two ruined castles and a large country house, the residence of the 5th Marquess of Normanby. You can walk through Mulgrave Woods – outside of the four-month shooting season, of course.

The Cleveland Way passes through Sandsend. Walking north along the old railway track there's still evidence of the 17th century alum industry, vital to the industrial revolution and significant in the growth of the village. The mines closed in 1871. The Middlesbrough Union Railway from Whitby to Redcar ran through here from 1855 to 1958, with the northern section reopened in the 1970s as a freight line for the Boulby Potash Mine near Staithes.

Yorkshire is packed with surprises. Sandsend is certainly one of them.

A dream cottage in The Valley

69

Swing Bridge A crossing point of the Esk since the 14th century. The present electric swing bridge opened in 1909

WHITBY

For setting, sights and sensations, Whitby takes some beating.

Part port, part holiday resort, it's fabulously situated in a gorge created over millennia by the River Esk which flows through the town and out to sea. Tightly packed buildings climb up the hillsides on either side. A century-old swing bridge separates the upper and lower harbours and also the old and new towns. The old side – East Cliff – is crowded and richly atmospheric. West Cliff is more spacious and elegant, with fine rows of sweeping terraces, built across the clifftop during the 1850s.

Whitby is rich in geology, history and literary connections. Captain Cook embarked on his many famous journeys from here and it became an important fishing and whaling centre. Whale blubber was once used as fuel for the streetlights.

It's the furthest north of the main North Yorkshire coastal towns, and the only one to face north.

Access to Whitby is straightforward. The train station is located yards from the harbourside. Driving into the town can be slow at peak times but you won't get lost. Parking is a different matter. The extensive car park by the station is the best bet and there's street parking on the North Terrace. There's also a car park within walking distance of the Abbey.

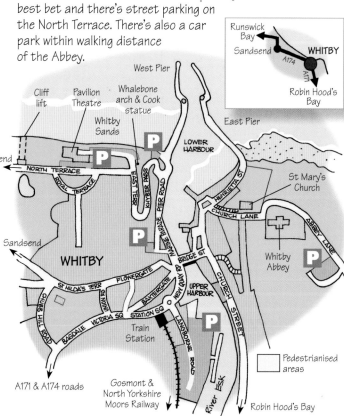

West Cliff from East Cliff

Pier Road on West Cliff has an abundance of cafés, restaurants, pubs, amusements and shops selling everything from clothes to souvenirs. It's also the fish quay where Whitby boats still unload.

George Hudson, who helped bring the rail link to Whitby, had the exotically named Kyber Pass cut through the rock in 1848 to provide access to his estates on the clifftop. He started to build the Royal Crescent to emulate the one in Bath, but went bankrupt with only half of it finished. The town's famous Whale Bone Arch was erected nearby in 1853 and has been renewed a couple of times since. The present bones came from Alaska in 2003.

The Magpie Café on Pier Road is one of Whitby's many fine fish and chip shops. You can't miss it – there's usually a crowd of hungry people queuing up the front steps.

The Magpie Café

St Mary's Church

The 199 steps

Whitby Abbey Founded in 657AD. Present one is the third on this site, built in 1220. Plundered in the 16th-century Dissolution of the Monasteries

East Cliff from West Cliff

East Cliff is a glorious medley of narrow streets, old cottages, ancient coaching inns and cobbled streets. A tiny market square was laid out in 1640 and the fairytale town hall built in 1788. It's all so perfect and atmospheric you could be walking in a film set.

The famous 199 steps climb steeply to St Mary's Church, an extraordinary building of various unfathomable styles going back to the 12th century, but still hugely attractive.

Nearby looms the great black skeleton of Whitby Abbey, forever tainted by the ghastly shadow of Bram Stoker's Count Dracula. While staying on West Cliff, Stoker was inspired by the view of the abbey to make it the setting for the Count's landing in England.

The old town hall

Whitby's two iconic harbour piers date back to before the 1500s. Originally of oak they were rebuilt of stone in 1735, each approximately 600ft (183m) long. Further additions to the west pier extended it to around 1,000ft (305m) in length by 1814. In 1905, both piers had 500ft (152m) extensions added.

Each pier has two lighthouses – an attractive one of stone and another not so good-looking. The west pier lantern stands on an elegant fluted tower, 83ft (25m) tall, built in 1831. To a different design, but equally fine, the 55ft (17m) high east pier lighthouse was constructed in 1854. Both were replaced in 1914 by utilitarian lights mounted on legs. The east one shows red for port and the west green for starboard.

East Pier bridge link removed in 2001 after storm damage

West pier

1905 extensions

East pier

The harbour piers

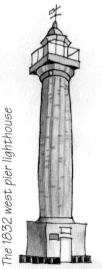

The 1832 west pier lighthouse

The 1854 east pier lighthouse

The 1914 replacement

The 1914 west pier replacement

The area is well-known for fossils, most famously the unique Whitby Jet, fossilised remains of the monkey puzzle tree. Black and shiny when polished, it became fashionable when Queen Victoria always wore jet jewelry after being widowed. In the 1870s there were 200 workshops and over 1,400 people employed in the Whitby Jet industry. It's still made on a smaller scale and sold in East Cliff shops.

With dramatic views, historic sites, stimulating architecture, the best fish and chips in the country, and boisterous seaside fun, Whitby truly has something for everyone – even Goths, who flock here to drench themselves in Count Dracula mythology.

Ravenscar

B1447 to A171
Whitby to
Scarborough
road

Footpath to
seafront

Whitby to
Scarborough
road

ROBIN
HOOD'S
BAY

Whitby

ROBIN
HOOD'S
BAY

A171

Scarborough

ROBIN HOOD'S BAY

The classic view from near the lower car park

No matter how often you visit this lovely village, the heartbeat always quickens when the famous view of the bay, the favourite of TV, print and calendar art editors everywhere, is revealed.

And that's before you tackle the precipitous main street, explore the maze of twisting lanes and alleys leading off, duck under crooked archways or clamber on worn stone steps to different levels.

That's the old part of the village, known locally as 'Baytown' or just 'Bay'. Obviously driving through it would be chaotic and mightily frustrating, so there are two car parks for visitors at the top of the hill in the Victorian half of the village. Road rage would be blasphemous at this blessed spot.

King Street and Ye Dolphin Inn

During the 18th century Robin Hood's Bay was a leading player in the vibrant smuggling trade, rife along the North Yorkshire coast. Most people in the village were involved and there's reputed to be a network of subterranean passageways linking the houses.

These days the village is a scenic paradise, an extravaganza of sandstone-walled houses and red pantile roofs. There are small shops, cafés, tearooms, pubs, B&Bs and hotels.

The crumbling cliffs bear witness to the violent storms that this part of the coast suffers and a substantial seawall has been built to protect the precious village. The beach isn't a bucket and spade classic, but when the tide goes out arcs of flat rock are revealed, a rich source of pool life and fossils.

As you leave this romantic and evocative place you may be thinking, as I invariably do, 'I'll be back'.

Old coastguard station

Bay Hotel

Robin Hood's Bay from the beach

SCARBOROUGH

Undisputed Queen of the North Yorkshire coast and the regional capital, Scarborough can seem big and brash on first appearances but behind the swagger there's a lively cultural scene, some fine architecture and a long history. The setting is appropriately grand and spectacular, with two wide bays separated by a dramatic headland, added to which there's an extensive ruined castle, once a powerful royal fortress.

The South Bay is where all the traditional seaside action is, with a magnificent beach, donkey rides and all the slot machines, fairground thrills, ice cream kiosks and fish and chip shops that any holiday-making family could ever want – and more. The North Bay also boasts a fabulous sandy beach, but it's quieter and has fewer facilities.

Scarborough has been an important port since Roman times. It's famous fair inspired the song *Scarborough Fair*, and after mineral waters were discovered in 17th century it became a popular spa town, attracting the prominent people of the day.

The arrival of the railway in 1845 brought yet more visitors. New hotels and smart houses were built and Scarborough's status as a fashionable seaside resort was assured.

Now a large town, Scarborough continues to attract the crowds, drawn not only by the seaside attractions but also by the beautiful parks and gardens, the museums, a good range of shops and restaurants, and several fine theatres, including the internationally famous Stephen Joseph Theatre.

The Scarborough seafront from Vincent's Pier

Dominating the town, the extensive castle walls occupy a vital strategic position with steep cliffs on three sides and a narrow point of entry. There's been some sort of fortification here since the Iron Age. In the 13th century it was one of the most important royal castles in England. The massive keep is 12th century, the Barbican 14th century, and there's also a Roman Signal Station.

The castle was badly damaged during the Civil War after being under siege for five months and suffered further destruction from German naval bombardment in 1914.

A potent mix of turbulent history and breathtaking views make the castle a fabulous place to visit.

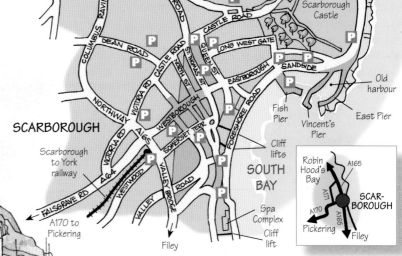

Car parks in Scarborough are plentiful and positioned close to most of the popular locations. However, a sunny day will attract many visitors and the parks soon fill. The central shopping area is pedestrianised and there's a large pay-and-display, on-street parking zone.

The aptly-named Grand Hotel stands imposing and grand on the South Bay clifftop. Four massive towers rise over the ornate six-storey building, which was the largest hotel in Europe when it opened in 1867. There are three cliff lifts around the Bay with the one down to the Spa, opened in 1875, the first cliff railway in England. The elegant Cliff Bridge was originally a toll bridge opened in 1827 for the fashionable people of the day to promenade across to the Spa. The Rotunda was built in 1829 and is now a local history museum.

This is a lovely, leafy part of Scarborough, with a fine view of the sea, and terraces of Victorian cream-coloured villas and hotels sweeping along the Esplanade.

A foul-tasting spring discovered beneath the South Bay cliffs in 1626 was declared to have magical healing powers and Scarborough began its rise as a popular spa town. Eventually a stone 'Gothic Saloon' was built around the spring in 1839, and a concert hall and gardens soon followed. Sadly this was burnt down in 1876 but the modern complex of a grand hall, now a conference centre, and The Spa Theatre date from the rebuild of 1880.

Donkey rides along the beach

The Rotunda and Cliff Bridge

The Grand Hotel and cliff lift

The Vikings founded a port here but it took until 1252 for a timber and stone harbour to be constructed. After further enlargements, by the 18th century Scarborough was one of the busiest ports in England.

The West Pier, where the fish market now stands, was rebuilt in 1820 to create a new harbour. Most fishing boats now moor at the North Wharf, rebuilt in 1926. Vincent's Pier, across the harbour, dates from 1752 and its famous lighthouse from 1804, although it was badly damaged in the 1914 German naval bombardment and largely rebuilt.

The lighthouse on Vincent's Pier

The Vickers gun

There's a number of curios around the harbour. A striking statue of a woman remarkably balaced on tiptoe and about to dive stands at the end of Vincent's Pier. The Diving Belle, erected in 2007, represents Scarborough in the 21st Century, moving confidently into the future. Another statue by the same sculptor, Craig Knowles, which stands in the town centre, depicts a Victorian female swimmer and represents the town as the UK's first sea-bathing resort.

A 1914 Vickers gun was raised by Scarborough Sub-Aqua Club and local fishermen in 1982 from the wreck of SS Hornsund, a British cargo ship sunk by a German torpedo on 23rd September 1917, two and a half miles south-east of its present location on Scarborough harbourside.

Scarborough richly deserves its position as Yorkshire's top seaside resort and is always worth visiting, though don't expect to be able to include all its many attractions in a day's visit.

The Diving Belle

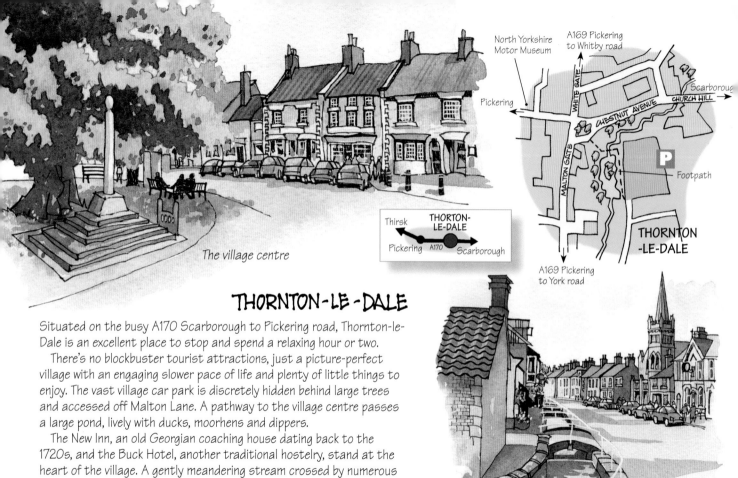

The village centre

North Yorkshire Motor Museum

A169 Pickering to Whitby road

Pickering

Scarboroug

WHITE GATE

CHURCH HILL

CHESTNUT AVENUE

MALTON GATE

P

Footpath

THORNTON-LE-DALE

A169 Pickering to York road

Thirsk

THORTON-LE-DALE

Pickering A170 Scarborough

THORNTON-LE-DALE

Situated on the busy A170 Scarborough to Pickering road, Thornton-le-Dale is an excellent place to stop and spend a relaxing hour or two.

There's no blockbuster tourist attractions, just a picture-perfect village with an engaging slower pace of life and plenty of little things to enjoy. The vast village car park is discretely hidden behind large trees and accessed off Malton Lane. A pathway to the village centre passes a large pond, lively with ducks, moorhens and dippers.

The New Inn, an old Georgian coaching house dating back to the 1720s, and the Buck Hotel, another traditional hostelry, stand at the heart of the village. A gently meandering stream crossed by numerous small stone bridges winds along the roadside. Seats on the triangular green are shaded by a single glorious tree. Picture-perfection indeed!

Malton Gate

Thornton-le-Dale has a remarkable range of independent shops. There's a general store run by the same family since 1856, plus bakeries, cafés, teashops, arts & craft shops, a pharmacy, a garage, a hairdresser, an antique shop – and more.

Almshouses on Chestnut Avenue (even the street names are picturesque) were built in 1670, a gift of Lady Lumley who owned much of the land around this area.

Thatched Belle isle Cottage beside Thornton Beck is said to be one of the most photographed scenes in England. You can also visit the North Yorkshire Motor Museum, a fine collection of classic and vintage cars, commercial vehicles and motorbikes on Pickering Road.

There's a great sense of community in the village, with the annual show in August attracting up to 15,000 spectators.

Thornton-le-Dale is one of those places that's a real pleasure to spend time in, but maybe sadly reflect afterwards, 'Why can't other places be more like that?'.

Bell Isle Cottage alongside Thornton Beck

The Buck Hotel and shops along Chestnut Avenue

PICKERING

Set at the intersection of the A170 and A169 York to Whitby roads Pickering is branded 'Gateway to the Moors'. It's reputed to be the oldest town in the district, dating back to 270 BC, founded by Peredurus, King of the Brigantes. These days it's a lively market town and busy transport hub with a wide range of shops, pubs, tearooms and eateries.

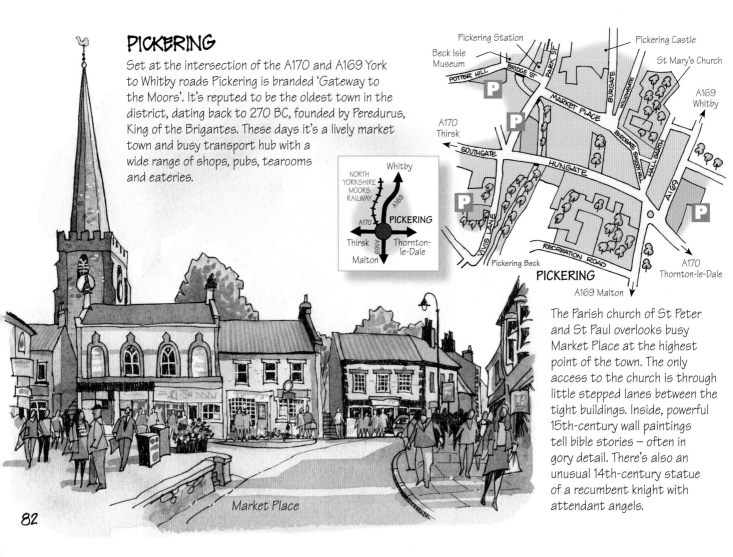

NORTH YORKSHIRE MOORS RAILWAY

Whitby

A170 Thirsk

A169

PICKERING

Thirsk

Malton

Thornton-le-Dale

Pickering Station
Beck Isle Museum
Pickering Castle
St Mary's Church
POTTER HILL
BRIDGE ST
PARK ST
A170 Thirsk
MARKET PLACE
BURGATE
WILLOWGATE
A169 Whitby
SOUTHGATE
BIRDGATE
SMIDDY HILL
HALL GARTH
A169
HUNGATE
VIVIS LANE
RECREATION ROAD
Pickering Beck
PICKERING
A169 Malton
A170 Thornton-le-Dale

Market Place

The Parish church of St Peter and St Paul overlooks busy Market Place at the highest point of the town. The only access to the church is through little stepped lanes between the tight buildings. Inside, powerful 15th-century wall paintings tell bible stories – often in gory detail. There's also an unusual 14th-century statue of a recumbent knight with attendant angels.

Pickering is the southern terminus of the North Yorkshire Moors Railway. Entering Pickering Station is literally stepping back in time, as extraordinary efforts have been made to recreate how a steam railway station used to look.

Luggage on the platform, gas lights, clocks, signage, advertising and a footbridge are all in period. There's even an absence of no-smoking signs. (A cover-all notice outside meets modern law requirements).

The crowning part of the project came in 2011 when the original 1840s roof, which British Rail removed in the 1950s, was recreated with a £500,000 replica. Of course there's also the big beasts themselves, the great steam locos with authentic carriages and rolling stock.

The past is also recalled at the Beck Isle Museum of Rural Life, which features a number of period displays of local shops and businesses with artifacts from centuries of collecting. There's also a Victorian-era pub and parlour plus a historic costume gallery.

The White Swan on Market Place

There's not much to see of Pickering Castle, a rudimentary early Norman 'motte and bailey' type fortification. It didn't see much military action but there's extensive views from the raised mound of it's 'motte' section.

Pickering isn't all about the past though. There's some good shops and Pickering Beck still winds attractively through the town. It's reckoned to flood on average every five years and last burst its banks in 1999. So if you're visiting during a rainy period, better pack the wellies.

Pickering Station

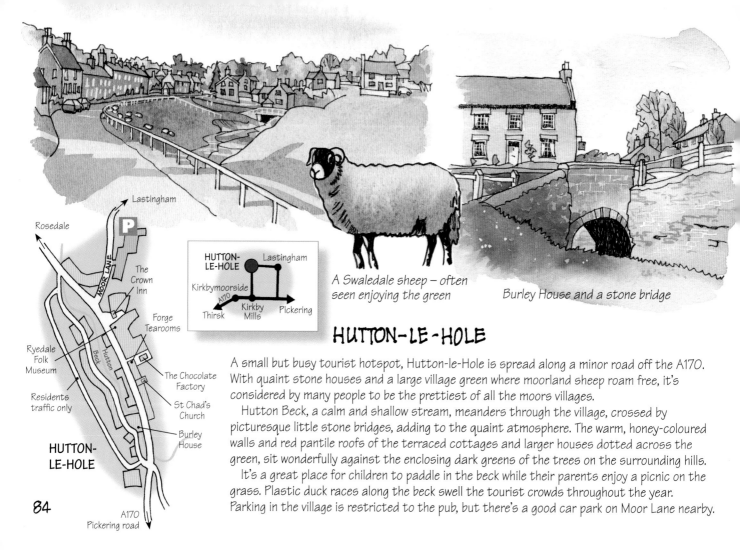

A Swaledale sheep – often seen enjoying the green

Burley House and a stone bridge

Map labels:

Lastingham

Rosedale

P

The Crown Inn

Kirkbymoorside

HUTTON-LE-HOLE

Lastingham

Thirsk

Kirkby Mills

Pickering

Forge Tearooms

Ryedale Folk Museum

Hutton Beck

The Chocolate Factory

St Chad's Church

Residents traffic only

Burley House

HUTTON-LE-HOLE

84

A170 Pickering road

HUTTON-LE-HOLE

A small but busy tourist hotspot, Hutton-le-Hole is spread along a minor road off the A170. With quaint stone houses and a large village green where moorland sheep roam free, it's considered by many people to be the prettiest of all the moors villages.

Hutton Beck, a calm and shallow stream, meanders through the village, crossed by picturesque little stone bridges, adding to the quaint atmosphere. The warm, honey-coloured walls and red pantile roofs of the terraced cottages and larger houses dotted across the green, sit wonderfully against the enclosing dark greens of the trees on the surrounding hills.

It's a great place for children to paddle in the beck while their parents enjoy a picnic on the grass. Plastic duck races along the beck swell the tourist crowds throughout the year. Parking in the village is restricted to the pub, but there's a good car park on Moor Lane nearby.

Hutton-le-Hole is home to the multi-award-winning Ryedale Folk Museum, Yorkshire's leading open-air museum. Set in three acres by the roadside, it consists of 13 historic buildings depicting the lives of ordinary folk from earliest times to the present day. They are all genuine rescued and reconstructed buildings including, shops, thatched cruck cottages, an Elizabethan manor house, barns and workshops, plus reconstructions of an Iron Age settlement and a Victorian classroom. There's lot's of hands-on crafts for children to try and special events are held throughout the year.

The Shop on the Green and the ice-cream shop

The village has a fine real-ale-and-food pub, the Crown, a couple of tearooms and a village shop. To tickle your sweet tooth visit the Chocolate Factory behind the Forge Tearooms, where you can watch chocolates being made.

St Chad's Church was built in 1934 and is dedicated to one of the three brothers who founded Lastingham Church as a Celtic Monastery in 654AD.

The green at Hutton-le-Hole and common land in the neighbouring village of Lastingham belong to the Manor of Spaunton, one of the few remaining Courts Leet in the country. The role of the Court Leet today is to protect Manorial Land from unsuitable development and generally keep things how tourists like us like to see them. At Hutton-le-Hole and Lastingham they are doing a splendid job.

A desirable home on the green

85

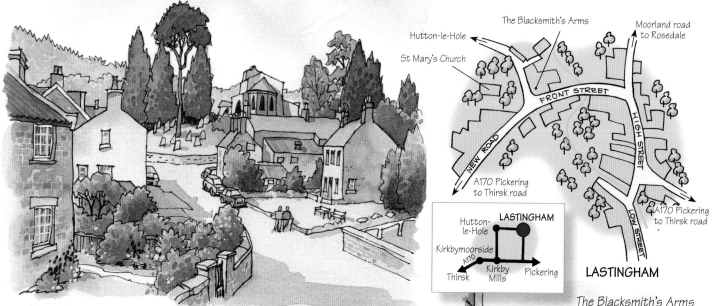

Front Street and St Mary's Church

The Blacksmith's Arms

LASTINGHAM

LASTINGHAM

Another pretty as a picture village, Lastingham quietly nestles in the steep-sided valley of Hole Back. There's no obvious visitor attractions, just a beautiful peaceful village set in glorious surroundings with open moorland on one side and woodland and farmland on the other. A moorland-fed stream gently tumbles through the village between tiny greens and attractive, well-kept stone cottages, bright with red pantile roofs much as they were centuries ago.

Lastingham comes within the medieval manor of Spaunton, still active in its land management through the Court Leet. Several farmers have grazing rights and sheep roam freely through the village. There's no public car park or shops, but you can park with consideration on the streets and near the pub.

Apart from its magnificent surroundings, the village's greatest treasure is the striking church on a mound, St Mary's of Lastingham.

It's been a religious site since St Cedd of Lindisfarne founded a monastery here in the 7th century. The present building dates back to 1078 and has a squat west tower with an apse – a semicircular extension – at the east end overlooking the pub.

Most unusually, there are steps down from the nave to a Norman crypt, as long as the church and still used for worship. It's a truly remarkable space of rough stone walls and four squat pillars supporting the nave above. St Cedd is buried next to the altar, which is lit by a tiny stained-glass window set into the wall of the apse.

Thousands of pilgrims are drawn here each year and to sit quietly in this place for a while can be a profoundly moving experience – even for a non-believer.

St Mary's Church

Low Street

The Blacksmith's Arms is squeezed on a corner by the church. It dates back to the 17th century and retains many original features.

It also has a lively connection with the ministry. The Reverend Jeremiah Carter was once hauled before his superiors for playing his fiddle and dancing in the pub on the Sabbath, and in the late 18th century it was kept by the curate's wife to help eke out the stipend of £20 per year and keep the couple's 13 children.

Today's pub is a lot more peaceful with its signature steak pies proudly advertised as being served in 'proper Yorkshire portions' (large).

NORTH YORKSHIRE MOORS RAILWAY

At 18 miles long, the North Yorkshire Moors Railway is the second-longest heritage line in the United Kingdom. It crosses the moors through fabulous scenery not accessible by modern cars, from Pickering to Grosmont, operated and staffed entirely by volunteers. Construction of the route, first planned by George Stephenson, took from 1832 to 1849. It was closed in 1965 when Dr Beeching's 'axe' fell, but the York Moors Historical Railway Trust reopened it in 1973.

The effort to keep everything authentic is impressive, not only in the steam locos and rolling stock but also the stations, which are all period pieces. You can dine in a Pullman coach and there are special events throughout the year.

Grosmont station

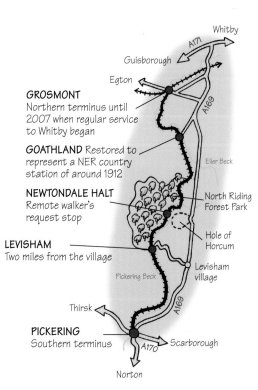

Whitby

A171

Guisborough

Egton

GROSMONT
Northern terminus until 2007 when regular service to Whitby began

A169

GOATHLAND Restored to represent a NER country station of around 1912

Eller Beck

NEWTONDALE HALT
Remote walker's request stop

North Riding Forest Park

Hole of Horcum

LEVISHAM
Two miles from the village

Levisham village

Pickering Beck

A169

Thirsk

PICKERING
Southern terminus

A170

Scarborough

Norton

Trains run every day from the beginning of April to the end of October, and on weekends and selected holidays during the winter (with no services from 24–27 December). Trains are mostly steam-hauled but heritage diesels are occasionally used. The line carried around 350,000 passengers in 2009.

HOLE OF HORCUM

Hole of Horcum from the car park

Driving across the moors on the A169 road from Pickering to Whitby you can't miss the Hole of Horcum. It's a huge bowl in the ground 400ft (122m) deep in places and about three quarters of a mile across. Green meadows carpet the floor, with woodland lining one side and moorland heather the other. Levisham Beck flows fetchingly through the centre, and it's been suggested that gradual erosion from it over the millennia may have created the Hole.

Other more creative theories have been put forward for its formation. Local legend has it that Wade the giant scooped up earth to throw at his wife during an argument but missed and created the nearby hill called Blakely Topping. This is generally discounted outside of licensed premises.

It's not even clear where the name came from. However, the Hole is definitely prime walking country, open and breezy. Various rights of way descend into its depths and around the perimeter rim. A popular circular walk crosses the moor to Dundale Rigg and Lastingham then returns high on the other side of the valley.

There's a handy car park situated across the road from the main entrance point to the Hole. Don't miss it!

FYLINGDALES

Radomes 1992

RAF Fylingdales on Fylingdales Moor is part of the UK and USA early warning system of a missile attack. Erected in 1962, three 130ft (40m) diameter 'golf balls' (radomes) became a tourist attraction, with motorists crossing the moor turning on their radios to hear the radar interference.

Alas, the system was upgraded in 1992 and the beautiful golf balls were replaced by something resembling a huge radio speaker off the back shelf of a 1970s teenager's car.

It's worth the aesthetic downgrade though – we still haven't suffered a ballistic missile attack.

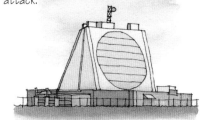

Solid State Phased Array Radar 1992

GOATHLAND

Set 500ft above sea level and with sheep grazing across its vast green areas, Goathland is a pleasant but rather ordinary moorland village. What is remarkable is the unfeasibly large car parks and the large number of tourists clicking cameras and pointing at a number of the old-fashioned buildings. Peaceful Goathland turned into a busy tourist attraction when it became the setting for the popular TV series *Heartbeat*, which ran from 1991 to 2009 in 18 series and 372 episodes .

With a traditional pub, a couple of hotels, a garage, a few shops and handsome village houses, plus wild moorland and a steam railway nearby, Goathland was the ideal location for the series, set in the 1960s. Credibly, stardom as Aidensfield hasn't changed the village that much and its period looks are what still draws the visitors.

Main Street, Goathland

Goathland Hotel (Aidensfield Arms in Heartbeat)

St Mary's Church

Goathland village is strung out in a long sweeping 'L' shape, with a great sense of space. Houses at the southern end are set well back from the road behind extra-wide grass verges.

The origins of the village date to Viking times, but as a religious site back to the 11th century. The present St Mary's Church was completed in 1896 incorporating artifacts from its Norman and Saxon origins. The church occupies a lonely site on the edge of the village before the road sweeps higher onto the moor.

The nearby railway was originally part of the Pickering to Whitby line, closed in 1965 but reopened as the North Yorkshire Moors Railway. An earlier line, horse-drawn on the notorious Beck Hole incline, passed through the village by the Goathland Hotel, and is now a fine walking route between Goathland and Grosmont.

Goathland Station, like all the stations on the heritage line, is a wonderful period piece, representing a NER country station of around 1912. It appeared many times in *Heartbeat* and also featured as Hogsmeade Station in the first Harry Potter Film.

Goathland Station

91

MOORS MOTOR TOURS

The Pickering Round. Approx 53 miles
Wild moorland and the unspoilt Esk valley

From Pickering take the A170 to Thornton-le-Dale (p80). Head north from the village on a minor road to join the A169. Pause at the Hole of Horcum (p89) then cross Fylingdales Moor and swing sharp left onto a minor road to Goathland (p90). Continuing through the village, pass the church and climb through open moorland to Egton Bridge, a peaceful village with a free car park, a railway station, a historic church and a good pub, The Postgate. A stone bridge over the Esk was washed away by floods in the 1930s, but rebuilt in 1992 in the style of the original.

Continue on the series of minor roads twisting and climbing through pasture and woodland along the delightful Esk Valley to Castleton. Turn left beyond the village, signed 'Rosedale' and climb to an elevated unfenced road with sweeping moorland and valley views on both sides. After about three miles, turn left past a small car park to Rosedale Abbey, now a popular tourist village but once the site of an austere 12th-century Cistercian Priory and centre of the vibrant Rosedale iron ore industry in the 19th century.

The bridge at Egton Bridge

Continue along Alder Carr Lane (signed 'Pickering') and after about four miles turn right for Lastingham (P86) and Hutton-le-Hole (p84).

A minor road takes you to the A170 and back to Pickering (p82).

Rosedale Abbey – the 19th-century church and ancient priory remains

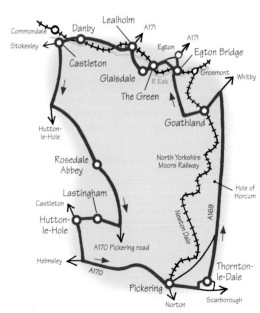

Sea and Scenery. Approx 40miles

The coast and the far north of North Yorkshire

Leave Whitby on the A171 and take the B1447 to Robin Hood's Bay (p74). Select Thorpe Lane out of the village and climb to take in some incredible views back to the coastline.

Turn left along the A171 and take the next right, the B1416 signed 'Sneaton'. After about a mile turn left onto a minor road signed 'Sleights'. Just before the village turn left to Grosmont, a hive of industry in the 19th century, quarrying stone, smelting iron, making bricks and servicing the railway. Competition from elsewhere gradually destroyed local industry and by the end of the century Grosmont had reverted to its original rural roots, though it's still well-known these days as the junction of the Moors Railway and the Esk Valley Line to Whitby.

Drive on through Egton, famous for its cosy moors' pub, the Wheatsheaf, and the wall paintings in the Roman Catholic St Hedda's Church. Join the A171 and head north to pass Scaling Reservoir. There's a car park at each end and it's a pleasant spot to stop and enjoy the water setting.

Just beyond the reservoir, turn right onto a minor road to Easington and join the A174. Head east, passing Boulby Potash Mine, just a small part of the vast chemical industry which dominates this part of North Yorkshire. Roads off the A174 go to Staithes (p64), Runswick Bay (p66) and Sandsend (p68) before returning you to Whitby (p70).

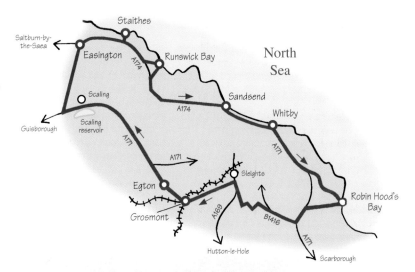

Grosmont Station

AUTHOR'S NOTES

Yorkshire geography

North Yorkshire covers an area of 3,341 square miles, making it the largest ceremonial county in England. The majority of the Yorkshire Dales and the North York Moors lie within its boundaries, and around 40% of the county is National Parks.

The landscape of the Yorkshire Dales National Park is a network of U-shaped valleys gouged out of the underlaying carboniferous limestone by the action of water and ice. Where the limestone abuts millstone grits, water cascades off the impervious grits and dissolves the limestone creating the elaborate caves, waterfalls and limestone pavements which abound throughout the Dales.

In contrast, the North York Moors lay on a complex mixture of shale, sandstone and coral limestone laid down by Jurassic tropical seas. This has created a typical moors landscape of heather-clad uplands slashed by deep and verdant valleys with substantial areas of woodland. It looks natural but it's actually largely a man-made and carefully managed landscape, with farming in the valleys and grouse shooting on the moors.

Where are the Yorkshire boundaries?

The vast span of Yorkshire was traditionally broken down into the three ridings – West, North and East Ridings – with the enclave of York in the middle. This setup survived invasions, battles and social changes for hundreds of years and in 1889 the Ridings were formally recognised as administrative counties for the purposes of formal government.

This lasted until the 1974 Local Government Act, which abolished the Ridings, hived off bits of traditional Yorkshire to neighbouring counties and added parts of other counties to Yorkshire. The new area was then divided into a jumble of smaller administrative counties and grouped under the four general titles of North, West, South and East Yorkshire.

After more tinkering, protests from Ridings' conservationists and a review of the boundaries in the 1990s, the East Riding of Yorkshire was restored as a 'ceremonial county name' which has only added to the immense geographical confusion.

It's a matter of debate what effect, if any, these extravagant boundary changes have had on the county's population. Yorkshire has always been a state of mind rather than just a physical entity. Loyalty and pride in the name is as strong as ever amongst Yorkshire folk

The Yorkshire Anthem

It's unofficial, but 'On Ilkley Moor Baht 'at' is widely accepted as THE Yorkshire paean, especially when played outdoors by a brass band. The song is thought to have been composed by a Methodist church choir while picnicking on Ilkley Moor and based on the old hymn tune, 'Cranbook'.

The lyrics vary and can become ribald when sung in licensed premises but the basic story is of a man freezing to death on Ilkley Moor because he's not wearing a hat (on Ilkley Moor bar the hat). A sad tale, but typical of the dry Yorkshire humour.

Ingleborough and a limestone pavement

Sheep

Intrinsic to the Yorkshire landscape, sheep have shaped the hills and fields, supported the farms and necessitated the building of dry stone walls and enclosures across the dales and moors. They are widespread throughout Yorkshire's country regions, some even strolling along village streets as if they own the place. In a way, they do. Many sheep are crossbreeds, bred for their hardiness in adverse conditions, but the purebred Swaledale has the honour of being the official symbol of the Yorkshire Dales.

Dry stone walls

They're a distinctive part of the Yorkshire landscape, and (naturally) the county has more dry stone walls than any other. According to the Countryside Agency, Yorkshire has around 18,900 miles of them, enough to enclose the whole of Britain's coastline.

Most walls date from the 18th or early 19th centuries, built to mark the boundaries of common land and to keep livestock in – or out. They were constructed without mortar or cement, relying instead on the weight of each carefully placed stone to keep the wall upright. Some are effectively two walls with through stones to bind them together and the space between filled with loose rubble.

Foot & Mouth Disease

Although Cumbria was the hardest hit, the outbreak of foot and mouth in 2001 also decimated farms across the northern half of Yorkshire. There were 139 confirmed cases and more than 50,000 cattle and 300,000 sheep were slaughtered before the outbreak was defeated. Dead animals were piled in huge heaps for mass burials and burning, witnessed on TV by a horrified nation. Visitor numbers plummeted, many small farms never recovered and Yorkshire's rural economy was slashed by a fifth.

But, ever-resourceful and with help from the government's Emergency Fund, Yorkshire's rural community fought back, farmers diversified into bed & breakfast or farm shops, tourism is again buoyant and lessons have been learnt from the outbreak. There have been some foot and mouth scares since but none on the scale of the 2001 catastrophe.

Long-distance walks

Yorkshire's wild open spaces are prime walking country. The Dales National Park has over 1,300 miles of public footpaths and bridleways and the North York Moors boasts over 1,400 miles.

A number of important long-distance routes pass through the county, including The Pennine Way, The Trans-Pennine Trail, Coast to Coast Walk and The Dales Way.

The Flat Cap

Although it's sartorial influence has spread worldwide, the flat cap, together with whippets, pigeons and knotted scarfs, is the iconic symbol of the stereotypical Yorkshire working-class man.

The classic cap is made from wool or tweed, with a little brim at the front and a higher peak at the back. It has been dated back to the 15th century but was *de rigueur* during the 19th and early 20th century when most working-class men wore one virtually all the time – even, it's said, in bed!

Yorkshire Pudding

An essential part of the traditional British Sunday Roast, Yorkshire pudding is made from a batter of eggs, flour and milk and served piping hot with beef and a plateful of vegetables. Traditionally, the pudding batter is spread flat on a dish and baked on a shelf underneath a joint of roasting meat, so tasty juices can drip into it.

These days the pudding has become a meal in itself, cooked in large dishes and poured full of gravy, stew, curry or any number of weird and wonderful combinations. Add sausages to the mix and it becomes toad-in-the-hole, another Yorkshire favourite.

Modern cooks tend to make the pudding in small, muffin-sized portions, an aberration to Yorkshire traditionalists, as are the low-fat, frozen versions sold in supermarkets.

Brass bands

They're not exclusive to Yorkshire of course, but the melancholic sound of a brass band can, for most of us, instantly conjure up a picture of windswept dales and misty moors.

Members of the original bands were usually workers in the local mines, mills or factories, often living in small mining towns and villages with less entertainment than the cities and where communities were more close-knit.

As Yorkshire industry declined, so did the number of brass bands but sponsors now support a credible number and they're hugely popular throughout the county and beyond. Rivalry between the bands is intense and culminate at the National Brass Band Championships held each year at the Royal Albert Hall, London.

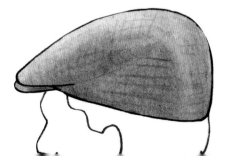

Also in the Sketchbook series...

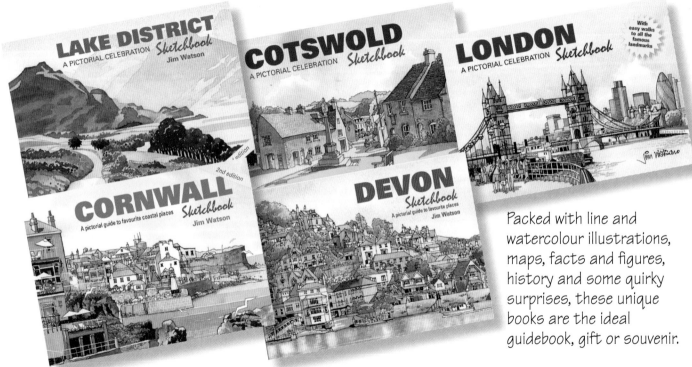

Packed with line and watercolour illustrations, maps, facts and figures, history and some quirky surprises, these unique books are the ideal guidebook, gift or souvenir.